The L

You can find out more about Kate, and sign up to her newsletter by visiting her website at www.kategallowaysmith.com

Also by Kate G. Smith

You've Got Mail

THE LOVE NOTE

Kate G. Smith

This edition first published in Great Britain in 2021 by Orion Dash,
an imprint of The Orion Publishing Group Ltd.,
Carmelite House, 50 Victoria Embankment
London EC4Y 0DZ

An Hachette UK Company

1 3 5 7 9 10 8 6 4 2

A CIP catalogue record for this book is
available from the British Library.

ISBN (Paperback) 978 1 3987 0914 0
ISBN (eBook) 978 1 3987 0297 4

Typeset by Born Group
Printed and bound in Great Britain by Clays Ltd, Elcograf S.p.A.

www.orionbooks.co.uk

To my daughter, Ariana, my world.

Chapter One

'Is it bad form to flirt at a funeral?'

I vaguely recognise the loud voice as I lean against the wall away from all the mourners. I watch the man at work and see a head of dark curls, familiar long ago, looking as unruly now as they were when he was a cute fifteen-year-old. My stomach drops.

Surely not! Why is he here?

The last time I saw the back of that head was as I was dragged away from it almost seventeen years ago at Sally Morton's summer party. Now he has the gentle, confident swagger of a football captain, the way he is leaning with one arm on the mantelpiece, trapping his prey who looks more than happy to be there. It's the swagger of an alpha male who should come with a neon sign saying, 'lock up your daughters'. His target hasn't noticed the swagger or the bright lights; either that or she is caught in them like a rabbit and is blissfully unaware of her impending doom.

'Oh, Nick, stop it,' the girl giggles, obviously not wanting him to stop.

Nick? It *is* you!

Nick Forster. My not-so-secret crush. A boy who used to stay behind in class because he enjoyed being there, certainly not this neighbourhood Tom who is purring so loudly I think he might self-combust. When did he become the cool cat of Haverley, the small town in Norfolk I had escaped from as soon as I could – and want to again right now. I feel as if I don't know *anyone* in the room, and I can't exactly go up to people and ask them who they are. A funeral is not the time or place for mingling. And it is certainly not the place to be flirting.

I roll my eyes at Nick's persistence, shuddering at the thought of being single, let alone being single and hit on at a funeral of all places. As if the thought of cold, prone bodies, teary spoken poems, and 'Abide With Me' could make anyone feel randy!

My sister, Gwen, is doing the rounds amongst the mourners, thanking people for being here, crying real tears when the guests offer their condolences for our mum who drank herself into an early grave. I knew my mum, which means I also know their condolences must be as real as the champagne Gwen is offering them.

'What do you mean, you want to pass around the Buck's Fizz? Like at a wedding?' I had asked her. 'What are *you* celebrating, Gwen? She liked *you*!'

She had hissed in my face and cried some more.

I had drawn the line at a buffet.

Gwen has the room covered. No one will notice if I sneak off. As the younger daughter, I've always been good at keeping a low profile and I really don't want Nick to spot me and come and talk to me. Today is not the day I want to be reminded that I am a heartbreaker as well as the black sheep of the family.

My hand hesitates on the doorknob. Mum's room was her sanctuary and I haven't been inside since I was banished as a child for spilling her loose powder all over the carpet in a game that may or may not have involved a teddy's seaside picnic. Where else was I supposed to find sand in the middle of the Norfolk countryside? As an adult, Mum's cutting tones and scathing side-eye still made my heart stop for a fleeting second. But she's dead now – and the dead can't look down their noses at the living, can they? Not from that angle.

The smell of her perfume, lingering long after she has vacated, hits me right in the stomach. But that's not what clasps a hold of me and drags me inside. Through the bedroom, into the dressing room that Gwen and I used as a den before Mum banished me and Gwen decided I was her mortal enemy, I can see a swathe of white gauze.

No!

I inch forwards, afraid that I might be right. But it is there, in all its glory, hanging in the middle of the wardrobe like a great big knife into my heart. Mum's wedding dress. The one she told me was missing only a few weeks ago when I asked her about it, thinking Ed might be about to propose because our anniversary is impending. It's there. Right there, like a shrine to Miss Havisham, only with less cobwebs.

I step carefully into the room, my feet with a life of their own walking me towards it. I reach out a hand to stroke it; the lace is stiff and cold, the sewn-on embellishments hard and sharp. Trust Mum to pick a dress as welcoming as she was. Pinned to the waistband, like a dry-cleaner's tag, is a thin piece of paper, yellowing with age. I untack it carefully, the paper ripping slightly at the punctures, and flatten it out to read it. It's a handwritten note and the blue ink has bled slightly into the fingerprint of the parchment. It reads simply:

E, je t'aime. LS x

E? Elizabeth, my mum. LS? Could be anybody.

Bloody mother, I think, and I burst into tears.

Chapter Two

'You never told me Nick Forster had turned into some sort of action hero with a jaw to rival Captain America. I barely recognised him.' I sit cross-legged on the flat roof outside my old bedroom window, my tears long dried up.

Squeezing out the double-hung sash windows had been a darn sight harder at thirty-two than it had been when I was a teenager. But I had followed the smell of vanilla tobacco wafting down the corridor from my mum's room and around into my old bedroom. Flashbacks of my best friends, Phillip and Perdita, nearly decapitating themselves on the window, struggling to get out before my mum noticed they were smoking, made my stomach turn to liquid as I opened the door to my old room and saw the pair of them sitting out on the roof waiting for me.

'Oh my God!' Perdita screeches at the mention of Nick's name. 'I know, right? He's gorgeous, grown well into his looks – and some.'

Phillip laughs and I coax out of my oldest friend what has happened to the quiet boy from high school who I not-so-secretly had a massive crush on.

'His jawline and the way he has that girl entranced *at a funeral* makes me think he's probably got a rep as a Haverley Boris Bike,' Phillip says knowingly.

'A what?' I snort.

'Come on, you're a Londoner now.' Phillip speaks as if

he's auditioning for a part in *Oliver!*, elbow dance included. 'A Boris Bike. Access for everyone, the first thirty minutes free, otherwise he's yours for twenty-four hours for a small fee of a broken heart and probably a case of the clap.'

I lift an eyebrow. *Surely not my Nick?*

'Or, you know? Maybe not,' Phillip adds, shrugging his shoulders. 'Maybe I'm just jealous.'

My heart sinks at the thought, then I remember Nick *has* just been hitting on someone at my mum's funeral.

'Oh,' I say, taking the roll-up from Perdita and drawing deeply on the vanilla tobacco.

I am about to add that he certainly looks good enough to be a local community asset, but I'm rendered speechless because I can't breathe.

Nope, still not a smoker.

'Will you never learn, Burnett?' Phillip says, peeling the roll-up from my spasming fingers and drawing on it himself. 'Still trying to inhale the bloody things even though you're not cool enough.'

'It's my mum's funeral,' I cough. 'I can smoke if I want to. And drink until I'm passed out over the loo. And hop on the Haverley bike if I feel like it, which I think I do – he's lush and he made my bits go tingly when I saw him!'

I feel light-headed and invincible and totally not at all myself because I've been necking fake champagne since I arrived back at my mum's house this morning.

'Don't be a dick. You've got Ed. People would kill for what you and Ed have, you're so hopelessly in love.' Phillip makes a gagging sound. 'Wind it in. You're drunk and emotional and don't want to end up with chlamydia – how would you explain that away to Ed?'

He's always to the point, is Phillip, that's why we're such great friends. The three of us have been best friends

5

since middle school. Then Perdita had gone off to Oxford to study medicine and can be found these days tweaking the noses and breasts of people with more money than sense – her own words. She is the sort of cool who hangs out in the Groucho Club and doesn't surreptitiously want to photograph all the people in there because she knows what they look like naked and unconscious. Draped in Dalmatian fur (faux) and sky-high Louboutins (real), with a white-blonde bob, she looks as out of place as ever and I love her for it.

Phillip, on the other hand, has never left Norfolk, except for his family's annual holiday to Minorca. He had got weirdly attached to our local village as we were all preparing to leave for university and is now married with a young daughter and living in a chocolate-box cottage on the outskirts of the village, writing horoscopes for women's magazines under the pen name Myrtle Marigold. He's dressed appropriately for a funeral; it is just his wayward orange hair and slightly dishevelled shirt that makes him look like a member of the Weasley family having just returned from battling Voldemort and not the upstanding member of the community that he actually is.

'Seriously, though, Mags, you don't really want to take the bike out for a ride, do you?' Perdita asks, taking the roll-up back from Phillip. 'I thought you and Ed were happy? You're what we all aim for in our *hashtag* relationship goals; don't ruin that by putting the image in my head that you want to go somewhere else! Every time I go on a first date, I hope it'll end up in a relationship like the one you guys have. Mostly, anyway. Sometimes I'm just hoping for some fun where nobody mentions butt play or ball gags.'

I sigh and lean back on my elbows. The heat is making the tar on the roof sticky. I have no idea how many Topshop skirts I ruined by sitting out here in the summers of my youth, but now I'm older I am slightly more cautious to avoid the glistening black spots underneath me.

My head swims with champagne and cigarettes.

'No, of course not. I was just ruminating,' I say. 'I love Ed, he's my rock; I literally have no idea what I'd do without him. And even after thirteen years, he still makes my bits tingle, too, sometimes, and that's not just from the thrush I get wearing the tiny polyester knickers he still thinks I like.'

We all curl up in hushed giggles. I love this about my best friends. We barely see each other these days, even though Perdita and I are both in London and Phillip's only a two-hour train ride away. What with work, life, relationships, trying to decorate a flat that has mildew because of the damp patches that the landlord can never see when he comes around to inspect, there is never any free time to do the other important stuff. Even so, when we get together, we always revert right back to our comfortable teen friendships.

'Thank you for coming today, guys,' I say, when I stop laughing at the point happy tears threaten to become sad.

'Don't be ridiculous, it's your mum's funeral, of course we were coming,' Phillip says, twirling his empty glass by the stem. 'It's weird, isn't it? I mean, it's your mum's funeral. I thought we'd be in our sixties with grandkids of our own and happily whiling the day away pottering about in the shed when our parents finally popped it. Not early thirties.'

The mood quietens as we mull over Phillip's drunken philosophy.

'I guess this makes me an orphan of sorts now, doesn't it?' I feel the weight of his words and the softness of the love letter from Mum's dress I had tucked into my cleavage.

'I wonder if your dad will come crawling out of the woodwork now your mum's gone,' Perdita says. 'He might be after a bit of this – and seeing as they never got divorced, he's entitled to it.'

She motions to the large house underneath us, but the mention of the word divorce has my eyes leaking again.

'I asked her if I could borrow her wedding dress once,' I say, picturing the pristine dress hanging pride of place in her room. 'Recently, too, not in a dressing-up way when I was younger. I thought maybe I could wear it when Ed and I get married.'

'What? What haven't you told us?' Phillip interrupts.

'Nothing,' I say, smiling. 'But you never know, do you? It's our anniversary in a few days and I think he might have a surprise up his sleeve because he's been acting a bit strange, secretive almost. And a girl can dream.'

Perdita stretches up to the sky; her Dalmatian fur looks hot in more ways than one.

'I didn't think you wanted to get married?' she says. 'I thought that was one of the things you were just *in sync* about?'

I cringe as Perdita says *in sync*. Phillip laughs. I'd been hit by the love bug as soon as Ed and I had locked eyes over a bar in the Cambridge club, Fifth Avenue. Me with my blue WKD, Ed with his snakebite and black, both of us with the innocence and excitement of freshers' week. We'd locked lips soon after, hips a few hours later, and had been inseparable since. At the time I had been one of those annoyingly in love people who banged on about finding the right person at the right time and how all my friends would see that soon enough. My university friends had been too intent on creating a wall chart of how many people they'd snogged and deciding which member of S

8

Club 7 they were to be interested in settling down with the right person. I had soon found myself spending more and more time with just Ed, and in our second year we moved into a flat we only had to share with each other. I don't see many people from my university days anymore.

'I don't necessarily *want* to get married but, you know, it'd be nice to have the same surname as our kids,' I say, only half-teasing my friends. 'Anyway, Mum said she had no idea where her old wedding dress was and I really only asked because I wanted her to be a part of my day in some form or another, because who knew if she would even turn up? But I've just seen the bloody thing hanging, pride of place, in her dressing room with a love note attached from what could be my father. Way to kick me in the teeth from beyond the grave.'

Perdita places a sun-warmed hand on my arm.

'I am so sorry, Mags. I know she wasn't always the nicest person in the world, but she was still your mum, and mums are supposed to be there unconditionally,' she says, sitting up and giving my arm a squeeze. 'You know you've always got us; you won't be alone just because you've got no family left. *We'll* never leave you.'

'Thanks, Perdie,' I say, my throat thick with emotion. 'But don't forget about Gwen.'

Phillip and Perdita groan in unison. I feel a twinge of loyalty to my older sister.

'Like Perdita just said,' adds Phillip, 'now you've got *no* family left, we're here for you more than ever.'

The window rattles and Gwen herself pokes her head out, her hair lacquered with so much hairspray it barely moves when she bashes the beehive on the upper sash.

'What are you doing out here?' she says in her usual clipped tone. 'Oh, you're here, too, are you?'

She eyes up my best friends, who she seems to loathe more than me; no mean feat.

'Nice to see you, too, Gwen,' Perdita waves coquettishly. 'So sorry about your mum.'

Phillip just ignores her.

'Gwen,' I say, 'I'm just taking a minute; I'll be back down before any drunken uncles start the "Agadoo".'

'It's our mum's funeral and you're out here acting like a teenager. Smoking and drinking.' She nods towards the empty glasses and the ash and stubs collected in the only flute that remains upright. I feel guilt eat at my insides. 'While I'm downstairs tending to our guests and holding the fort, as always. Even Ed is being more help than you are, and that's saying something. Grow up, Maggie. Why can't you just forgive Mum for dying and act like a normal human being for once?'

I bite my lip and shrug an apology at my friends. Gwen is right, though I would never be caught saying that out loud. I brush the rough bits of asphalt from my dress and follow Gwen's head as it disappears back into the house.

Chapter Three

'You're late.'

I sigh and try to pull a smile on my face.

'Only a few minutes,' I say, shrugging, slipping out of my jacket and sliding into the chair at my desk.

I boot up my computer, ready to get on with whatever fun copy is thrown my way at Procter and Rowe this morning. I often wonder, on my less busy days, whether Mr Procter and Mr Rowe decided to set up a PR company because it was what they were good at, or because it was what their initials spelt out. I can probably hazard a guess given the collective social repute of our clientele. Still, it doesn't do well to disparage one's employer, especially when I'm not yet trusted with my own clients, I'm just given everyone else's copy to write up when they're too busy – read: *can't be bothered.*

'A few minutes add up if you're late every day for a *whole week.*'

Oh! You're still there.

My boss flips the dark curtain of hair out of his face in a movement that belies the fact the haircut went out of fashion before I was even born and was never in fashion for people over the age of puberty, which he must have hit, even if it was only a few years ago.

'My mum has just died,' I huff, staring up at him and hating myself for using that as an excuse. I'm tired and getting up every morning this week has been difficult, so he's lucky I'm in work at all.

He doesn't even blink. The rest of the team have hushed to a deathly silence. All listening but pretending not to.

I feel my ears heat as my eyes prick with tears.

Not now, Maggie. Be strong. Be strong.

'You had the funeral last weekend.'

I baulk.

'So, I'm supposed to be over the fact that she's dead just because she's scattered over the waters of the Norfolk Broads, am I?' I know I am shouting now but I can't seem to control the volume coming out of my mouth. 'Am I just supposed to get on with things? Forget she was even alive? Not everyone has the emotional intelligence of a gnat, Mr Duncan. We can't all be you.' I have no control over the words, either, it would seem.

Mr Duncan turns a shade of berry that matches his shirt rather well. Kudos to him, though, he's managing to keep his cool.

'Perhaps you'd like to step into my office, please, Margaret.'

It's not a question. He hasn't called me Margaret since I accidentally uploaded some inappropriate photos from my personal stash to a client's Instagram account. Nothing naked or inflammatory – I've been with Ed for far too long to be sending him selfies of my wobbly bits, and his idea of sending me wood would amount to a picture of wonky shelves he's proud of. No, this had been a screenshot of a meme I wanted to send to Perdita and Phillip of a cat playing a banjo with a pithy comment about sacking off work to follow your dreams. In all fairness, I thought the picture worked quite well with the ethos of the company I'd accidentally uploaded it about, but it turned out I was the only one who thought so.

'Look, Maggie.' Mr Duncan seems a bit more at peace with himself now he is safely tucked away in his office that smells like a pro-wrestlers' dressing room, with the after hint of stale coffee. I eye up the spare chair but stay standing. 'I know this has been a very difficult time for you. I can't imagine losing a parent. But we are a business. Proctor and Rowe expect the best from their workers.'

I can picture the middle-aged men in their chequered sweater vests that barely cover their paunches. Whenever they come into the office, they have the added sheen of sweaty excitement that comes with being in a room full of women, most of whom are under the age of thirty. I think Proctor and Rowe were hoping for a lot more than *the best* when they hired the giggling girls straight out of university with no PR qualifications whatsoever. It was a hard truth the day I realised that I had been hired for my looks rather than my acuity and intellect garnered by three years studying English and American Studies at a low-key university. And now, when I catch sight of myself in the office microwave, I look less bombshell, more bomb-wrecked.

Mr Duncan is still talking. 'And we can't afford to have someone who is not on their game. We think maybe it's best if you took some time out.'

I snort out a laugh. He surely can't be sacking me for being half an hour late?

'You're giving me my P45?' I ask, aware that Mr Duncan doesn't look like he's joking.

'No, of course not. We can't sack you for being late . . .'

Didn't think so, I think, relieved.

'But we can ask you to take some time away.'

I feel sick. This is so unfair. I am here, a week after scattering my mum's ashes, and Mr Duncan is sending me away because I'm not up to my job. A job that I could do with my eyes shut because it is both tedious and idiot-proof in equal measure.

'Don't be silly, I'm perfectly capable of doing my job,' I retort.

Sweat is gathering under my hairline. *Don't send me home, I need to stay busy.*

'That wasn't a question. We are a PR firm; we need to protect ourselves against negativity and sloppiness. Nothing is sacred anymore; nothing is private, is it?' He waves an arm around as if his stuffy office is the big wide world. 'With the internet and social media. We can't afford to not look our best. Our face is our business.'

'So now you're saying it's my face that's the problem, not my work?' I can feel my problem heating with the embarrassment of being told I'm currently not pretty enough by a man who looks like a greasy teenager and is at least ten years my junior.

'No.' His arched eyebrows and pinking face discredit his words. 'We're just thinking of *you*. We want *you* to be OK, and at the moment we don't think you are.'

I'm fine. I'm sure I'm fine.

'Just take a couple of weeks, that's all. And come back to us fresh-faced and ready to go. Maybe get a haircut or your nails done as a treat to yourself. You never know, it might help your well-being.'

'My well-being can look after itself, thank you,' I say, my voice getting higher pitched with each word. I have a love/hate relationship with my pre-Raphaelite autumn-coloured curls. I don't need Mr Duncan telling me to get a haircut to know I need a haircut.

'Come back on the first of October, think of it like the start of a new school year.' Mr Duncan claps his hands together and stands up from his chair.

Our meeting is over; I have to work quickly.

'What about my copy for Janet?' I say, pleadingly.

'It's sorted already; I've got the junior on it and she's already downloaded some stock photos for the article. You don't need to worry about your work while you're gone.'

They had this planned! The junior? The girl with a glossy waterfall of chocolate-coloured hair that falls all the way past her gravity-defying boobs. *Nothing to do with my face, hey?*

'Oh, and Maggie,' Mr Duncan says, louder now the office door is open, 'clear your desk before you go; we don't want your mouldy mugs festering while you're gone.'

'Oh, shut up, Robert, you knob!'

I catch sight of myself in the window of a Savers, reflected amongst the rows of reduced bottles of shampoo, knock-off shower gel, and cheap wine. I fit in quite well with my frizz-ball of a head, cheeks like the red apple-scented bubble bath, and a shirt dress that had looked hip when I spotted it in the local Oxfam, but now looks like it belongs to a fat man.

I wonder if I should get an Uber back to Bexley from the office in Peckham, picked for its proximity to London City but with cheaper rent. Shoving my box of belongings onto one hip I rummage around in my bag for my phone and check my bank balance . . .

I clamber off the bus with my work life still tucked under one arm and the street I live on looks warm and inviting. Ed had picked Bexley because of its low crime rate and, handily for him, his accountancy firm is based in the centre of Bexley Heath. So, by way of bargaining, I had picked this road because of its wisteria-clad frontage. Our flat, the ground floor of a red-brick terrace house, has its own front door that is clambering with the stuff, beautiful for a few weeks in May, then green and twiggy for the rest of the year. I thread the key into the lock and push open the door with my free hip.

Luckily, I have a good few hours to bathe before Ed gets home. I can shave my legs and armpits and at least distract Ed from the fact I've been semi-sacked by offering him some sexual treats. I'm pondering the effectiveness of a blow job when a high-pitched squeal bursts from the far end of the flat.

I drop my box on the hallway table and check through the door to the living room to make sure I haven't inadvertently broken into someone else's home.

Nope. There is the old brown saggy sofa and the gigantic flat-screen TV.

So why is there someone squealing in my bathroom?

Oh God, maybe someone is being murdered in there?

I pick up an old copy of the Yellow Pages, mouldering under the hallway table with the letters no one wants and a few years' worth of dust. It's heavy enough to maim if I throw it with the spine outwards.

The squeal turns guttural. *Am I too late?*

I edge down the hallway, past the open door to our bedroom. My head turns at the strewn duvet. *I could have sworn I made the bed this morning.*

I keep walking, the noises strained now. With just the kitchen between me and the intruders, my heart is racing. Then a weirdly familiar male voice joins in, *'Yeah, baby, is that good? Have I hit the spot? Shall I go harder?'*

I stop on the spot, immediately embarrassed by what I'm hearing. It's not murder, it's sex, just sex – bad porn-style sex if the moans and groans are anything to go by. Cringing, I let out a sigh of relief and turn to put the Yellow Pages back before anyone sees me with it and asks what I'm doing.

Then the realisation hits.

Chapter Four

I clench my fists, now hoping that the weird noises *are* coming from intruders who have broken in just to make use of my bathroom. My mouldy, damp, unattractive bathroom that makes me feel grubby even if I've wallowed in a bubble bath until I'm wrinkly.

It could be true. More likely to be true than walking in to find Ed with another woman, surely? My stomach contracts. Whoever it is in there can't be with Ed: she is having far too much fun.

'Yes, yes, that's it, don't stop.'

Ed is very much a man with vanilla tastes that don't stretch all the way to the bathroom. Not until he's finished at least, then he is always first to the bathroom even though I've drummed into him the importance of my post-sex wee to fend off any urinary infections. No, it can't possibly be Ed in there. My heart is beating so fast I think it might bump its way up my throat.

'Ooooohhhhhhhh.'

That could have been either of them.

Nope, definitely not Ed, he isn't a moaner.

My hand is frozen on the bathroom door handle.

Do I want to do this? Can't I just walk away and pretend I was never here? Ed's not likely to be in there, I could just give these two people who are obviously really enjoying themselves their moment's fun and get back to . . . where? To work?

My stomach contracts even harder. I can't even escape back to work to get away from these law-breaking, indoor doggers. I've been forced out of my work and am now contemplating leaving home, there are no other options. No. Best just to get it over with. We'll all have a jolly laugh about how punitive it actually is having sex in my bathroom, then they'll disappear off into the sunshine, probably to find somewhere more romantic to finish off. Though it sounds like they might be nearly there now.

It'd be rude to interrupt really, wouldn't it? Not at this crucial moment.

The embarrassment of intruding on a couple in the throes of passion is gluing me to the old worn carpet just outside the bathroom. I am trying to picture anything other than what is going on in the tiny space with a dripping shower over a yellowing bath, a sink smaller than my childhood Barbie's bath, and a toilet that has a squeaky wooden seat with a nasty habit of sliding out from under me. But the visions of what could be going on are driving me crazy; that, and it is becoming difficult to breathe because my chest has restricted so tightly my diaphragm is suffocating me.

Shaking the tension out of my body just how my Pilates teacher had shown me in the one class I'd attended, I push open the door into something soft and yielding.

'Oh my God!' I gasp.

And the woman sitting on the sink opposite yells it right back at me.

'Oh my God!'

'Yeah, baby,' Ed says, as he kneels on the floor in front of the woman, apparently unfeeling of the door pushing at his feet, or the fact he has a long-term girlfriend.

Ed's head protects what is left of the unknown woman's dignity as I stare at her, unable to process what I am seeing.

A flicker of recollection pounds deep at the base of my brain. The woman looks mortified, her naked backside is perched on the edge of the sink, one impossibly long and tanned leg leans on the bath, the other is hooked over the towel rail. My favourite fluffy John Lewis towel is offering a soft perching place for her foot. The tumbler that holds mine and Ed's toothbrushes is almost at risk of being touched by a naked backside that belongs to neither of us. For a single, jaw-dropping moment I have to hold in a giggle. It is all too much to process. My love, the man I thought might propose today of all days, is here in our bathroom with his face buried in a naked woman's nether regions, something he hasn't done for years with me because he says I give his tongue cramp.

There is no way I am ever brushing my teeth in that sink again, is, weirdly, the only thought that crosses my mind as I resist the urge to lean over and rescue my night cream and floss before they succumb to the same fate as the toothbrushes.

The woman seems to regain her senses, wide-eyed, as she scrambles frantically, trying to pull her legs together, which is hard with Ed's head between them

'Stop!' she hisses, batting Ed over the head with a perfectly manicured hand.

'Ow, what are you doing? Why should I stop? What is it, did you just . . . you know?' Ed says, his voice muffled but unfamiliarly boastful.

'No!' the woman practically screams. 'It's your wife.'

Ed laughs. He actually laughs.

'What? I'm not married,' he says, getting up too quickly and stumbling backwards right into me. 'Ooof!'

The pain as Ed stands on my bare toes is sharp and quick and has more bite to it than the dull ache that has punched me hard since I opened the bathroom door. But it is overshadowed by the pain I feel when Ed catches sight of me in the mirror hanging over the sink. My world comes crashing down around me as his eyes widen in shock.

'No,' I say quietly. 'No, you're not married.'

It's ludicrous. This whole scenario is ludicrous. I wish it *had* been a bloodbath I'd walked into and not this. Anything but this. Ed and I haven't even had the two, five, or seven-year itches, we're simply Maggie and Ed. Ed and Maggie. As obvious and comforting as fish and chips, or maybe pie and mash. Beans on toast? We work together as a couple like a well-oiled cog, sometimes not even needing to open our mouths to communicate.

I feel bile rising up my throat at the thought of Ed's mouth now.

He is my rock. At least, I thought he was.

'It's not what it looks like,' he splutters, spinning on the spot and wiping his hand down his face.

He reaches out and grips my shoulders and I have to fight the urge to throw his dirty hands off my dress.

If looks could kill, then the girl scrambling down from our sink would have Ed gone in an instant.

'Did you trip and your mouth just happened to land on her vagina? Because I'm trying to work out how this is not *exactly* what it looks like?' I say.

'Don't be so crude, Mags.' Ed is now looking at me like I've grown two heads. 'What are you doing home, anyway?'

I am trying really hard not to lump him one.

'Don't call me Mags! And don't blame me for being home and ruining your fun,' I yell, surprised at the force of my voice. 'I kind of got the sack . . . a *temporary* sacking,' I add quietly.

This is so weird. I am admitting to Ed what I'd been scared of admitting, and even in this most awkward situation I feel guilty telling Ed I've been asked to leave my workplace because I'm not up to the job. Yet here we are standing in our bathroom WITH A HALF-NAKED WOMAN and I'm the one feeling guilty.

Seemingly not having made enough of a mess of everything, the other woman pipes up.

'Ed, are you going to tell her?' she says, her voice as smooth as her legs.

I look between this gorgeous naked being and my Ed, eyes darting as though watching a game of tennis play out and not my life.

'Tell me what?' I splutter. 'Ed?'

Ed's face looks as though he's just come back from doing a Park Run. Dread is building in me. He turns to the other woman and I feel my world tilt at the way she looks at him. That's not a *quickie at lunchtime* look, it's an *I know you* look. A look I remember from when Ed and I first met, the annoying loved-up-couple look that Perdita had been jibing me about at my mum's funeral.

'My mum's just died,' I blurt, as though this could make a difference to Ed's moral compass.

It hadn't worked in the office, and it isn't working here. The only thing it is doing is reminding me of just how shit my life is right at this very second. The other woman bends down to collect her knickers from where she must have thrown them on top of the wash bin. There is an awkward – if it is possible to get any more awkward – moment where we all have to jiggle around one another to give the other woman space to leave the bathroom. Like a pack of lemmings trying to figure out the best solution. I ignore the obvious solution of me just leaving, but fear of my jelly legs not working properly stops me and the last thing I want to do is leave Ed alone with this woman, even if it is just for a split second.

How am I going to be able to leave him alone, ever again?

The thought makes bile turn over in my stomach. A washing machine of acid sloshing around with my breakfast.

'I'll see you soon, Ed,' the other woman says. She reties her dress and straightens it over her legs, scrunching her knickers up in her hand and heading towards the door.

Ed follows behind her and I'm behind Ed, staring at the back of his head that I know so well. Each swirl of blond parting, the way he's flattened down the tufts at his crown with gel, it's all so familiar. I want Ed to say something. Anything. That he won't be seeing this woman soon, that he has no idea who she is and what she had been doing sitting on his face. But instead he nods sheepishly at her whilst glancing sideways towards me. The woman slides into her shoes at the front door as I peer over Ed's shoulder.

Why didn't I notice them?

And she jiggles the door handle in the awkward way it needs to get it to turn.

Oh God, she's been here before.

Then she leans over to kiss Ed on the lips as she leaves. As though I'm not standing there watching. No Maggie at all. She kisses him. On the lips. It is too much for my brain to comprehend, it whirls like my stomach is. I reach out and clutch at the wall.

'What the . . .' I yelp as the door shuts quietly. Ed's shoulders slump and he takes his time turning to face me. 'What's going on, Ed?'

'I think we need to talk,' he says, finally.

Those fateful words.

'Too right we need to talk,' I splutter. 'Who *was* that?'

And then the penny drops. The other woman had been faintly familiar because I had met her last summer at Ed's staff party. Except back then she'd had a man on her arm, but I can remember vividly how gorgeous I'd thought this woman was, and how much I had coveted her dress.

'Annabelle,' I say, wounded, slipping down the hallway wall slightly.

There is a huge gap in my knowledge. When had Annabelle gone from attractive work colleague to sexual fiend and boyfriend stealer? No, wait! More importantly, but much harder to comprehend, when had Ed gone from dependable long-term partner, the man who took out the bins without moaning, even when there was bin juice involved, to absolute fucking traitor?

Chapter Five

'Here you go.'

Ed hands me a steaming mug of sweet tea. I cradle it between my hands as I perch on the sofa, unable to make myself comfortable.

'Why are you being so nice to me?' I ask, blowing on the hot liquid, not wanting to look at Ed because I don't want his eyes to tell me what I'm already starting to suspect.

That is the problem with break-ups. It is always one party that is certain, the other is just doomed to heartache and pain. Even in the best of break-ups there is always one who is pushing for it more than the other. Yes, I'm sure even Gwyneth Paltrow and Chris Martin in their 'conscious uncoupling' were uneven in their wishes to unhook themselves from each other like carriages on a freight train.

Urgh, Gwyneth. Gwen.

My sister has never been a lover of Ed. She has always looked down on him in that particular way she does which no one really notices except me. The unsubtle eye-rolling and louder than needs to be tutting.

'I'm being nice to you because I care about you,' he says, perching on the sofa next to me, but not quite close enough to touch.

The distance between us is as vast as a moon crater, with an anti-gravity repelling force to boot.

'You *care* about me?' I scoff. 'What about love? What about not hurting me? What about the promises we made each other that we would never, ever cheat? That we would be those kinds of couples that can talk about anything and not have to resort to turning to someone else.'

'Please can you not shout at me? I feel bad enough as it is,' Ed says, moving as far away down the sofa as physically possible without falling off. 'I never meant for this to happen.'

'I'm not shouting!' I shout. 'And stop vomiting clichés at me and tell me what the hell is going on.'

Ed opens his mouth and promptly shuts it again. Obviously, it is too hard for him to tell the truth.

'OK, let's start with this. How many times have Annabelle's flaps been in your face?'

'Mags . . . Maggie, stop it, you're just being rude now.'

'YOU DO NOT GET TO TELL ME TO STOP!' I am still shouting and I can't stop, my heart feels like it is seconds away from a cardiac arrest. 'You don't *ever* get to tell me to stop. Not ever again. Now tell me the truth. How long has this been going on?'

Ed fiddles intently with the skin around his fingernails. 'A while.'

I watch as Ed's whole body seems to sink further into the ugly brown sofa that I've always hated. He looks relieved. I don't want to contemplate what that means, but my brain has other ideas.

He's glad it's out in the open. Now he can go and live with Miss Perfect and not have to bother with Miss Hairy-Legs anymore.

'A while? So, you've been sleeping with lots of people, then?' A plea for it not to be something important enough for him to end our relationship. I am hurtling towards a conclusion that I just cannot cope with.

Ed shakes his head. 'No, just Annie.'

The familiarity shakes me to the core. My body quivers with the force of the hurt.

'I'm sorry,' he says. He looks like a child now, curled up into his own body, protected and vulnerable. 'I really never meant to fall for someone else.'

I want him to unfurl, to protect me when I need it, not himself. Tears flow down my cheeks.

'Fall for? You've *fallen* for her? How long has this really been going on – and don't say a while.'

Ed looks close to tears himself now.

'Since Barney's birthday party.'

Barney, another of Ed's colleagues. Barney's party with the swing band and the impromptu dance-a-thon, the sweaty way Ed had been flinging Annabelle around his dance space with the skill of someone who took classes while his other half worked overtime to try to quell some of the debt they'd accrued. Debt from their endless takeaways and holidays to try to stem the gut-wrenching pain of paying London rent for a one-bedroom misery hole.

I wrack my brains to think what had happened after the party, which is hard as the party was almost a year ago. A year. A whole year of lies and betrayal. It is like trying to remember a dream – the more I delve, the murkier the memories become.

'And have you . . . is she . . .' I can't think of the question I want to ask. What I need is for Ed to tell me the whole sordid tale from beginning to end in minute detail. 'Tell me how it happened.'

'Why? What's the point? It'll just hurt you more,' he says, his head in his hands.

I feel red-hot anger.

'You don't get to tell me what will hurt me more. I want to know exactly what happened, the wheres and hows and whys. If you don't tell me then I can guarantee what I am imagining will cause me even more pain. Don't do that to me.'

Ed sighs. The living room is silent except for the rushing of blood in my ears. This is going from a terrible, terrible mistake, a blip in our long-term relationship that we could have maybe ironed out over time, to a quantum change in both of our lives. I want to prolong the inevitable for as long as possible.

'We kissed, that night,' Ed says, exhaling.

He looks as though he is deflating. In front of my very eyes his body is deflating with relief. I could kill him right here and now if there was a suitable weapon to hand.

'What? When?' I gasp.

'You left early, remember? Said you had a headache and were going to head back for an early night.'

Visions flash in my head. The spinning, the dancing, the heat of the basement ballroom in Soho. Everything had been sweaty and exhilarating, half-lit with candles and the glow from the partygoers' faces. I had felt immediately out of place and downed a couple of gins for courage but all they'd done was drag me down even further. I'd looked on as Ed and Annabelle had taken to the floor like pros; everyone around me had been nudging each other and talking in those drunken hushed voices about how they were *obviously going to be at it later*. I'd had no choice but to get out. If regret is a cancer, I am now palliative.

'So, if I'd stayed then none of this would have happened? Is that what you're saying?'

Ed shakes his head. 'No! Maybe. I don't know. I guess.'

'Then we can get past this, can't we? If it was just a slip-up that happened because I left you in the wrong place at the wrong time, we can get past this.'

More silence fills the room. My sniffs are like thunder.

'I don't think we can.'

There it is. The final bombshell.

'But you just said you cared about me!'

'I *do* care. I really do care about you. You can't spend twelve years with someone and not care about them. I will always love you.'

Ed finally sits upright and gives me the respect of his full gaze.

'Thirteen,' I correct him, hope bubbling in me. 'So we can sort it out.' I am adamant now, Ed still loves me.

'I think even if you hadn't left the party when you did, *this* would have happened at another point in time.'

'*This* being your total and utter betrayal?' I spit, hearing the bitterness in my voice. I am done being kind. 'If you weren't happy with me then why didn't you just say? When we could have had a chance to work things out.'

'I tried,' Ed says, softly.

I don't think he is trying to make this any harder for me, but every time he opens his mouth, I feel my insides die a little more. I picture the times he'd tried to get me to sit down and have a proper conversation, the times I'd batted away his advances, the times we'd started to have an adult conversation but it had turned into something funny and superficial and light and we'd both come away from it laughing. Is this what Ed is talking about? Is it my fault that we haven't been able to have those deep and meaningful conversations that could have saved our relationship?

'You should have tried harder.' I can't help being anything but cruel now. Why should I be the only one hurting?

Ed looks in pain, too, but it can't be anything compared to the dizzying emptiness filling me.

'Let's not play the blame game, Maggie, please. You're amazing. You'll find someone who thinks so and you'll be happy, too.'

His words are like a knife through my heart.

'So you weren't happy with me? You don't want me anymore?'

Ed falters and my broken heart drops out of my chest.

'I think the word you are looking for is *no*,' I say, getting to my feet. 'Well, thank you for a wonderful thirteen years, Ed. Glad it's all come to this. Enjoy your life with Annabelle, I hope *she* makes you happy enough to not cheat on her. Will you be finding somewhere else to sleep tonight, then?'

I am still hoping that this is all a misunderstanding, that Ed will turn around and laugh and shout *April Fools'*, even though it is mid-August. Instead, he looks up at me with a face that looks ten years younger than it had a few minutes ago.

'Actually, Maggie, the tenancy for this flat is only in my name, you know, because of your credit rating back then. I think it's probably best if *you* move out. Sooner rather than later. Let's not prolong the pain.'

Another memory I had forced to the depths of my toes to never have to think about rises up again like a tidal wave. When we'd first met and been in the throes of blinding love, Ed had been a nightmare with money. He never had enough and it seemed to never be his fault either.

I can't pay my phone bill because I've been messaging you too much.

I drove into a parked car because I was thinking about you too much.

I spent all my wages in a week because I love you too much to not send flowers.

I hadn't questioned it. Who does in those early heady days of too much fun and not enough sleep? So, I took out the credit cards and signed up for the loans. We both spent the money, but only I took the hit when the debt came around to bite us. It isn't something I speak about, like ever, because it is too embarrassing. But it was over seven years ago; surely it doesn't count anymore, my credit is just as good as Ed's now.

'This is my flat just as much as it is yours – just because it doesn't have my name on the tenancy agreement doesn't mean I have to move out,' I say, hurting that he is making me take the sole burden of our historic debt.

'It does; I've already checked with the letting agents,' Ed says. 'You're going to need to move out.'

I reach out, blinded by tears, grab a faux lead statue of an angel I've always hated from the peeling sideboard that had come with the flat, and throw it at Ed's face.

Chapter Six

'There's a naked man dancing around your kitchen, Perdita,' I shout into my phone as I balance it between my shoulder and ear, my hands full of pretty much all of my life's belongings thrown into two heavy suitcases. 'Well, he's almost naked. It looks as though he's wearing your apron!'

Perdita splutters a mouthful of obscenities into my undefendable ear. 'That cost me a bloody fortune and he's rubbing his cock all over it. Fuck's sake. I'm going to have to burn it now. What's he doing, Mags? And why are you at my flat? We've both lived in London for years now and I can count on one hand the number of times you've ventured north of the river. Don't give yourself a nosebleed!'

I huff and let go of the handles of both suitcases so I can take the phone in my hand. Perdita is still swearing into my ear.

'Wait a minute. How can you see in to my kitchen? Have you climbed over the fence?'

Not technically, thankfully, not with lugging two great suitcases.

'Your gate was open,' I say, a half-truth if ever there was one.

Actually, I'd hung around the entrance to the locked gates until a hapless tenant had been leaving. Then I'd swooped like an eagle and got my foot in between the gate and the post before it clicked shut behind them. If anyone had been watching they would have been on the phone to the police faster than I could then work out how to get back to my bags without letting the gate shut. A few manoeuvres with a brick, an old pile of recycling bags, and a sticky piece of chewing gum that someone must have left on the bottom of the gate because the bin was at least three feet away, and I was through.

Perdita groans. 'I'll need to get on to the warden, that bloody gate is always open. I don't pay a fortune for ground rent just to have him spend it all on holidaying in the Algarve every five minutes.'

I feel a flash of guilt at the trouble the warden might get in if Perdita does dob him in for something he hasn't actually done.

'So, you're staring at Kristoff through the kitchen window now, are you?' Perdita asks.

And just like that my guilt is pushed aside by shame. I am standing staring at a naked man in an apron dance around my best friend's kitchen unawares.

'Oh, God, yes I am,' I say, blushing a deep red and glad again for the cover of night. 'And who is Kristoff? Is he your date for this evening? Shall I make myself scarce before I see you naked, too? I don't think my eyes could take it.'

'Piss off, Burnett,' Perdita says, joking as much as I am. 'My boobs would make you sing.'

She is probably right. They do seem to have an annoying habit of staying put and not succumbing to gravity like mine have. I temporarily forget I am on the phone and stalking a naked man while I contemplate the fact that Perdita's boobs might not be all that natural. Now probably isn't the time to be discussing that, though, and Perdita is still talking.

'I'm not at home. Airbnb, my friend,' she says. 'Kristoff often rents my flat while I'm away with work. Him and his Swedish buddies like to have parties. I thought they were posh parties with Camembert and red wine; I might have to rethink my options if he's just using my flat for his naked shenanigans – *that* privilege is saved for owners only! He's probably sitting on my sofas whilst naked, too, *blurgh*. I'll have to steam-clean everything.'

'Oh God, Perdie, there are more of them and they're *all* naked!' I shout down the receiver, squeezing my eyes shut so I don't have to look.

But it's too late, five pairs of male genitalia are burned onto my retina. No qualms at all about the heartache I've just been through.

'Can we help you?' a sing-song male voice asks.

'Oh God, Perdie, they've seen me,' I squawk into the phone, my eyes still firmly shut. 'What do I do?'

Perdita is no help whatsoever as she belly laughs into my ear.

'Go and join them? Just don't sit your naked arse on my new Laura Ashley.'

'Sorry, can we help? Only we heard you shouting from the kitchen and thought you looked in need of something,' the male voice sings again.

'Nope, nothing, nope, I'm fine. You can all go back inside now, no need to panic,' I say, hoping I am speaking in the right direction.

'No offence, but you look to be the one who is panicking,' he says, kindly.

'Nope, fine, all good here, I'm fine, perfectly fine.' As I say it I can feel my eyes well with tears.

All is *not* good here, is it? I'd spent the last few hours packing up all of my things as Ed had sat on the sofa engrossed in his phone and holding an ice pack to his nose once it had stopped gushing blood all over the carpet.

No doubt messaging Annabelle to tell her I'm on the way out because I'm a domestic threat.

Depressingly enough I had managed to fit all of my clothes, shoes, and toiletries into one of the two suitcases I own. There were no photos, or ornaments, or frippery gathered over time that I could pack in the other, and I didn't want to leave it for Ed, so I'd packed a few of my favourite books and told Ed I would be back for the rest. This was it. The total sum of the last thirteen years wasn't even squashed into two suitcases.

What else do I have to show for it? Heartache and a mountain of debt, both of which I'd have happily left behind, both of which seemed determined to come with me.

'Are you sure?' the man asks, gently. I peel open one eye and try to focus through the tears. 'I'm Kristoff, why don't you come inside? We're just about to eat, you can join us.'

'I'm Maggie. But you don't know me,' I stutter. 'I could be a serial killer, or a paparazzi, or something equally as hideous.'

'No offence again, but you don't look like either,' Kristoff says as I feel his arm wrap around my shoulder. 'Are you going to open your eyes and say hello? We won't bite.'

'Perdita, what do I do?' I shout into the phone.

'This is what you get for springing a surprise visit on me without checking it's OK first. And why *did* you come over? You never said.'

Kristoff swipes the phone from my hand in a move I could have prevented if I'd seen him coming.

'Hi, Perds, we'll look after her, don't worry.'

'Get some clothes on, you freaks!'

Perdita's tinny, shouty voice is cut off.

'I needed somewhere to stay, that's all. But I'll be on my way now.'

'Don't you have any family you can stay with?' he asks gently.

Which was quite possibly, unknowingly, the worst thing Kristoff could have just said. My tears start flowing like a tap again. I don't have any family to go to. Not unless I go and stay with Gwen. And, quite frankly, I'd rather stay with a bunch of gang-banging naked men than Gwen.

'Perdita will be home from Norfolk in a couple of weeks, you can come and stay then, I'm sure,' he adds, hugging me as close as is comfortable given his state of undress.

'Norfolk?' I sniff.

Kristoff nods. 'She's doing some work for BUPA in Norwich. Wouldn't tell us who she's fixing up though, as per. We took bets on it being Delia.'

I laugh, despite myself. A flicker of light is glimmering at the end of my tunnel of doom. Maybe, just maybe, I have a place to go after all.

'Look,' I say to Kristoff, feeling a bit silly for all my tears as I peel my eyes open, 'thank you for the offer to come in, but you've given me an idea. I'll get out of your hair now.'

My eyes fall on Kristoff's chest, the white blond hairs springing out from the sides of Perdita's – soon to be ashes – pinny, and feel my face go a deep red.

'It's a saying! I mean I'll leave you be,' I add quickly at Kristoff's wry smile.

'I know,' he says, grinning. 'I've lived in the UK for nearly ten years now. It's my naked friends who have travelled in for the gathering today.'

I shake my head and gather up my suitcases again.

'This has to be the weirdest day I think I've ever experienced,' I say, giving Kristoff another restrained hug.

'But tell me, Maggie,' he says, 'I bet it has been exhilarating.'

I contemplate his remark all the way to the tube station.

Chapter Seven

I push open the door, drop my suitcases, and flump down onto the old banquette in the hallway. Throwing off my shoes, the tiled floor feels lovely and cool under my achy feet. After two tube rides, a two-hour train, and a taxi that took longer than both of those put together, I am finally home. Not home home, but *family* home, I had reminded myself numerous times on the journey. I felt like a failure to be admitting to going home, but as long as I remind myself every so often that it is only temporary until I have somewhere else to stay in London, then everything is shiny and OK.

The key was hiding under the old duck-in-boots by the front door where it had always been kept. I did once have my own key, but I always defaulted to the duck because it felt weird letting myself into a house where I wasn't always welcome.

The silence around me feels eerie. It is one in the morning, so I'm not sure what kind of noise I had been expecting, but still, there has to be something to stave off the voices in my head telling me I am stupid.

It has only been two weeks since I was last here, when the house had been full of people I didn't really know, saying goodbye to a mum I hadn't really seen properly in over three years. And even that had been a fleeting visit for reasons I cannot contemplate right now. *The dress.* I wonder if it is still hanging pride of place in Mum's dressing room or if Gwen has tidied it away. I finger the small piece of paper that I'd found pinned to the dress which is in my pocket. For some reason I can't bring myself to part with it. As though E and LS's love can osmosise through my clothes and heal my broken soul.

Pulling myself to my feet, I trudge through the tiled hallway, past the closed doors to the living room, office, and dining room, and through to the large kitchen diner. This was the only part of the house Mum had really looked after and it is still pretty dire, but at least it is functional. Less Scandi than Perdita's flat is, but still a Hygge feel with its modern units, an island, and a dining table big enough to seat all Mum's friends. Big enough to seat family, too, but we never had the chance because we never had an invite. Bifold doors to the overgrown garden that I can't see in the dark take up most of the wall behind the dining table.

Flicking the side lights on, the room in all its shabby glory is illuminated just enough to keep the edge off the scuffed cupboards and marked paintwork. I know there will be no food in the house; Gwen had stayed in the days after the wake to clear out the *compostables* as she so pretentiously put it. I hadn't offered to help, knowing full well Gwen would have martyred herself even more than usual if I had. I go straight for the cupboard I know Gwen will have left well alone – the alcohol cupboard.

It isn't a normal kitchen cupboard, it is a pantry wall that looks like four separate doors, but when I pull the handle the whole of one side comes away with it. Lining the shelves are Mum's favourite pastime – vodka, brandy, whisky, home-made gins of all sorts of concoctions, decanters, crystal glasses, and silver trays to display it all on when she had fabulous parties that I wasn't invited to or even allowed to attend when I lived here.

It still feels wrong as I pick up the bottle of rhubarb gin and a sealed tonic from the cupboard. The ice cubes – *thankfully not compostable* – clink as they hit the bottom of the most expensive-looking crystal glass that I could find. I top the glass up with too much gin and a little tonic and sip.

Oh dear lord, that is good!

I cough.

And very alcoholic.

My throat tightens and my eyes prick with tears.

Nobody knows where I am. I could die here of fatal rhubarb gin poisoning and wouldn't be found until my own decomposing body resembles a stick of the stewed fruit.

I take another sip and laugh out loud at the thought of my pink, stewed body being found by Gwen of the sensitive disposition. She'd probably faint, then blame me for making her faint, even though I'm a big soggy dead mess on the floor. Blame is the forefront of Gwen's entire repertoire of emotions when it comes to me, and I have no idea from where it had first stemmed.

I take another sip and perch on the bar stool at the island. The wood of the worktop is warm to touch, which is nice because the rest of the house is freezing. The perks of the foot-thick walls of the old Georgian almost-mansion. It has never been a mansion in my eyes, just the house where I grew up. Besides, there are only five bedrooms and surely a mansion had to have at least ten to qualify for mansion status?

'Cheers,' I say to no one in particular, holding my glass up in the dimly lit room and downing the burning liquid.

I drink to the awful month of August. The month that saw me bury my mum and reopen old wounds about our

39

non-existent relationship. The month that saw me sent home from a job I had worked my backside off for due to the fact, for a few short weeks, I hadn't been working hard enough. A month that saw me walk in on my boyfriend with another woman.

The drink is going down easier with each salutation, the toast to each of my failings becoming more slurred until I stop saying them out loud and stop pouring into the crystal. The bottle will suffice for the last of the salutes.

'To Kristoff.' I swig. 'And his bunch of naked friends.'

'To my family home.' I choke a little on this one. 'And getting out as fast as possible.'

With the next swig the bottle is empty. I stumble off the stool and wobble a little on my feet.

Whoa, who's spinning the room?

The kitchen moves around me faster than I can keep up. Dropping to all fours, I crawl through to the stairs and drag myself up to my old room. It may not be mine anymore but it still has a bed and a small en suite for when my body decides the bottle of gin is a bad idea.

Wait, this whole house is mine now. It's all mine, not just my bedroom. Mum's bedroom. What lies waiting for me in Mum's bedroom?

It's almost too big to process on a churning stomach and a spinning head, but I skulk back out of my bedroom anyway.

Chapter Eight

With each crawling step I feel the trepidation tenfold. I pause for a moment outside my mum's bedroom door. It will only take a few seconds, just a quick glimpse and then I'll leave the forbidden room. Elizabeth Burnett may be dead, but her rules live on. My fingers grasp the cool, familiar doorknob and my heart starts to hammer through my T-shirt.

Apart from the blip at Mum's funeral, the last time I set foot through this door was as a child, twenty years ago, yet the scent of floral talcum powder mingled with Chanel draws me right back there like it was yesterday. Even then Mum's bedroom was a room that made my young skin prickle and the hairs at the back of my neck stand on end if I spoke any louder than a whisper. I flick the light switch. Nothing has changed. Feeling the ripple over my arms, I draw them around myself and hug my body tight.

Ceiling-height sash windows, dusky pink velvet curtains that pool over the thick carpet, a dressing table with trinket pots and creams, a walk-in dressing room full of evening gowns and real fur stoles full of dust; they all add to the mystique of what had been the most exciting room in the house when I was growing up. Probably due to the fact I was forbidden from it.

I'm not sure what I've been expecting. Something different? Something that I wouldn't recognise from those times when we'd all been happy as a family. The times before Mum started partying and drinking with friends until the early hours of the morning, then forgetting to get up and play school mum, so Gwen and I had been in charge of our own lunches and finding our way to the school bus half a mile down the road.

I can't really remember the good times, I had been too young, but there isn't a month that goes by where Gwen doesn't remind me of what we once had in a tone that implies she is superior because she *does* remember.

The hammering of my heart has tamed slightly, so I take a tentative step into the room, feeling, all of a sudden, coldly sober. The carpet is squashy and soft under my bare toes. The bed is still made, one corner of the duvet turned down, as though waiting patiently for its owner to return to lift it and climb in. A single sob escapes from me and I hold it in with the back of my hand.

'What am I doing?' I ask no one in particular, wondering if I should escape from here and go and curl up in my own waiting bed.

Then I look up and see the door to the dressing room is still open and I have a burst of bravery.

Away from the battle of the funeral, it is beautiful. A heart-shaped corset bodice with ivory lacework so intricate it looks as if little mice and bluebirds must have done it. A skirt so full I'm not sure how it is keeping its 3D shape with no body in it to propel it outwards. A simple diamond-encrusted belt dovetails the two.

My hands reach out and stroke the skirt, gently, as though it will vanish under my fingertips the way everything else in my life has been doing. This time it is soft and cool, silky and almost too delicate to be felt, a small pluck in the fabric a cry from where I took the note. The rest of the dressing room is a shambles; clothes strewn here and there, squashed into shelves without a care, not folded or hung. Hangers are left empty while dresses and shirts are dropped carelessly to the floor or draped over each other on the chaise that I remembered Mum 'rescuing' from an auction seller who was going to tip it after a bad day's sales. The memory is vivid, visceral. As though I am still there, holding my mum's hand in the cold, damp barn that had doubled as the auction room, the smell of Chanel and soap the only comforting thing as Mum had started shouting about the horrors of sending good furniture to the tip.

The man had argued with her – about what, I can't remember, I had been too young. I can just feel the same dread that had been heavy in my stomach watching the man's tweed cap almost fall off his head with the shouting. Mum, as always, had remained steadfast, calm; the wave of a hand or the touch of an arm.

Somehow, we had ended up back in our old car with the pink chaise strapped to the roof with ropes.

'That's how it's done,' Elizabeth had winked at me.

I had forgotten all about the chaise – its faded pink velvet and battered dark wood legs – until this very moment. I sit down on it with a thump, wondering why Mum had seemed so keen to get it when it is so bloody uncomfortable. But it is a memory. One of the few positive memories that I have. Time alone with Mum, when Mum enjoyed having me around.

I look back up at the wedding dress.

Why didn't you want me to borrow it, Mum? Was I really that untrustworthy? Did you think so little of me?

A thick ball of emotion lodges in my throat. *Damn you, Mum, and all of the times you ignored me in preference of your friends and parties – and anything as long as it didn't involve being a mother.*

And, as though my body is moving without any need for instruction, I throw off my jeans and T-shirt and lift the heavy dress down from its hanger. The weight feels good, real, as though it is a sentient being of its own. Tiny little hooks at the back of the corset are a disguise for a zip and, opening it up, I step into the dress and pull it up to my chest. Zipping it up is harder, but I am determined; in the end I have to twist it around and zip it closed at the front, then twist it back, but I am in. I slip my arms out of my bra straps and tuck them into the sides of the bodice, then pull my hair out of its messy bun and let my dark red curls fall around my shoulders.

'Screw you, Mum. It fits!' I say.

A mirror the size of a small car is leant against the wall. It is more shabby than chic, but through the dark patches of oxidised copper and silver nitrate, I can see myself. I look beautiful. Like something out of a fairy story, and this time I'm not the witch. The alabaster of my skin, my smooth collarbones and shoulders look radiant against the redness of my hair and the ivory of the bodice. The way the waist is nipped-in makes me feel like a woman, not just a fat lump of flesh and boobs and hips that I have felt for a while now. It is as though the dress has been made especially for me.

Is this why you didn't want me to wear it, Mum? Because I look so beautiful in it? I think, then chastise myself for being so ungracious and indelicate. Because I know my mum would have looked amazing when she wore this dress.

A thought crosses my mind as I swish the skirts around my ankles and wonder what shoes Mum wore with it.

What did you look like, Mum?

There are no pictures that I can remember seeing of Mum in this dress. No wedding photos at all, come to think of it. It was probably too much for Mum after Dad left the scene, maybe. Seeing photos of when they were happy might have tipped her over an edge that she constantly seemed to be precariously teetering on – I remember the times of shouting and crying more than the happy times. But then why keep the dress, if not photos? And why keep it so well preserved when all the other clothes look like Saturday closing time at a really expensive Primark?

Maybe there are some pictures stashed away with all the other family photos that don't adorn the house. Surely there must be baby photos of me and Gwen somewhere, pictures of our mum when she was young and happy, pictures of our dad when he was around? I have never once seen a picture of Dad, of LS; he was out of our lives before I came along.

There are so many places in the house that Mum could have kept old photos, so I have no idea where to start, or even if I want to. Instead, I turn back to the stained mirror and imagine Mum in the dress. Had it been the happiest day of her life? A time before she had the responsibilities of two daughters and no one to help her?

My phone shrills from downstairs where I must have left it in the kitchen, right underneath me now, loud enough to hear through the quiet of the night.

'Shit,' I say, wondering if I should just leave it. *But what if it's Ed?*

I gather up the skirts in my arms and half-run, half-walk down to the kitchen to see. The rustle of fabric is like the sound of heavy rain on a tin roof, only louder.

Don't hang up, Ed, don't hang up.

I reach my phone and answer it without looking.

45

'Ed?'

'Can you get out of Mum's room?' Gwen yells into my burning ear. 'And take that dress off before you damage it!'

Slamming the phone down, I scream into the kitchen. I grab the material of the bodice and force it around to undo it, pulling frantically at the zip.

What am I thinking? What am I doing here?

The thick heavy material is closing in on me, squeezing my chest and restricting my breathing.

'Get off!' I yell, panting. 'Get off!'

I yank as hard as I can until the zip comes loose. Ignoring the ripping sounds, I pull the heavy bodice down and step quickly out of the dress as it falls to the floor.

Stupid. Stupid. No wonder Ed's gone, you're so desperate. Look at you.

Shivering with cold and nerves, I sob into the empty space. I am a fool. I need to leave this place and its memories and get back to London to sort things out with Ed. I wipe my tears with the back of my wrist, guilty at the mess I have made of the once-perfect dress. I hook my arms back into my bra straps and take a deep breath to calm my racing heart.

Picking the dress up off the kitchen floor, I see that in my frenzy the inner lining of the bodice has ripped away from the whalebone.

Shit.

I move a hand over the tear I've made, lift up the flap of material and wonder if it is repairable. As I do so, my fingers catch on what feels like paper.

That's a weird thing to line a dress with.

Carefully, so as not to rip the bodice any further, I pull the flap of material back down and hold it out to make a small pocket. There, pressed between two struts of the

46

boning, is a small, folded piece of paper. It's similar to the note I already have upstairs in my jean's pocket.

E, je t'aime. LS x

I pull it out – it is thin with age and feels dry and weightless – and open it up.

E, Pour toujours à toi à partir de ce jour. LS x

I slump onto a dining chair and weep into the gauze until it is saturated with salty tears.

Chapter Nine

Oh no. Oh no no no. Please no.

The sun is streaming through the unclosed curtains and hitting me in the eyeballs despite my eyes being shut. I roll over onto my side to get away from the glare and immediately regret it. My head feels as though there is a drum and bass night going on inside it and I am the angry neighbour complaining about the noise. With a lurching stomach, I retrieve my phone from the floor where I dumped it after I fell into bed last night, the second bottle of home-made gin lying sadly next to it as a reminder that, whilst I may have been able to function after one bottle, two had definitely been my limit. I can feel the dull ache of a memory trying to press through the nausea, but I'm not quite ready to acknowledge that yet.

I unlock my phone and look at the damage.

> 2.54 a.m. *Hi Ed, just wanted to let you know I'm fine. I've moved out for the foreseeable future and will be contactable in the case of an emergency only.*

He knows this, he was the one to tell me to leave. Still, it's not a bad message. Strong.

> 3.09 a.m. *Ed, how do you feel about knowing I'm now the owner of a gigantic house and you can't share it with me? Good luck in the mouldy hellhole you're now probably sharing with Annabelle.*

Less strong!

3.11 a.m. *I will be willing to take you back if you promise to never do that again.*

Let's not ever talk about this.

3.13 a.m. *. . . but only if you wash your face with bleach first.*

I am never drinking again . . .

The gin is rolling around in my stomach like the ocean after a storm. I daren't read the rest of the messages in case they get worse. If that is at all humanly possible.

Why couldn't I have stuck to the first one? I think, swallowing heavily. *That would have left me looking almost in control.*

As it is, I am anything *but* in control. So out of it, in fact, that I can't stop myself from rolling out of the precarious position I am leaning at in bed and I hit the threadbare carpet with a thud. Ed hasn't replied to any of my twelve, *yes twelve,* messages.

'Somebody shoot me now, please,' I whimper, trying to stand up without losing my balance.

After a shower so hot it could have stripped the skin right off my bones, I feel slightly more human. I turn once again to my phone, deleting all but the first drunken message I had sent to Ed – there really is no need to have a permanent reminder of my ineptitude. My whole life is that on paper.

I refresh again to see if he has replied, making the mistake of scrolling through our past messages as I head down the stairs. The banal shopping lists, the silly play-fights, the loving notes, the pictures . . . oh, the pictures. I have made it all the way back as far as my phone memory will let me before I spot the wedding dress lying on the floor in the kitchen and the memories of last night come flooding back as quickly as the gin does. The dress. The notes. The call from Gwen. How on earth had she known what I was doing? I look around as I walk over to pick up the dress from where I had left it strewn on the floor, half-expecting Gwen to jump out and accuse me of ruining yet another thing in her perfect life. But the silence is only drowned out by my sniffing.

The weight of the dress feels accusatory this morning. How could I damage something so robust? The tear of the fabric gapes at me like a mouth and I pick the note up from where I must have thrown it onto the kitchen table with the first empty gin bottle.

E, Pour toujours à toi à partir de ce jour. LS x

I picked Spanish over French at school and through my layman's knowledge of that romantic language can read what the first note I found says. *E, je t'aime. LS x*. E, I love you. LS x. However, I can't even hazard a guess at this one.

But the sweet sentiment is almost lost in my gut-wrenching memories of Ed's wooing romance. He'd leave little letters, almost exactly the same as these, dotted around the flat or snuck into my pockets. Mum must have had a romance just the same, even the unhappy ending. I laugh ironically, stroking the soft paper on which LS had offered his heart to my mum.

Across the kitchen the alcohol cupboard is still as open as I left it the previous night and the vodka is calling. I contemplate swigging some just to take the edge off. But then I realise that might make me a borderline alcoholic and I don't want to inherit that from my mum or give Ed the satisfaction of making me destitute as well as heartbroken.

Instead, I grab my phone and flick to the besties WhatsApp group that I share with Phillip and Perdita.

*Friends, I have an emergency. I am currently at my mum's
house and need you to come over asap. I wouldn't normally ask but I am desperate.*

It isn't long before my friends reply.
Perdita:

*What's happened? I was worried about you after the na-
ked shenanigans last night. I'm working this a.m., but can
be over at three at the latest.*

Phillip:

*What nakedness? What have I missed? And Perdita, who
works on a Saturday?!! Crazy. I'm currently at a children's
birthday party with thirty five-year-olds at a park full of fi-
breglass dinosaurs. It's OK, though, there's a bar. I'll be
over as soon as I can, Maggie. Hope you're OK? Get the
wine in though.*

I smile at their replies and feel grateful at their eagerness
to help. The least I can do is cook them supper. There is
just the small task of shopping for some food first. Before
I can start Googling a recipe that doesn't involve cooking
for five hours but looks like a gastric delight, my phone
shrills in my hand.

'Gwen?' I answer warily. My sister never calls if it can be
done by email or text, or telepathically – which was her usual
means of communicating to me just how much she dislikes
me. And twice in less than twenty-four hours is unheard of.

'Glad to hear you're sober now, though looking no less
of a state than you were last night. What are you doing
at Mum's house?'

'Just needed a place to stay for a bit, that's all. A week,
tops,' I reply, looking around to see if Gwen is actually

hiding behind the curtains. 'It's a work thing,' I add quickly before Gwen asks why.

'Don't try on any more of Mum's clothes while you're there,' Gwen says curtly. 'Don't steal any of her stuff. Or even bother going through her papers – I'll do all of that in a few weeks. I've taken annual leave deliberately so I can sort through Mum's finances and organise things. I don't want you messing it up or *borrowing* from Mum without me knowing.'

'The thought never even crossed my mind, Gwen. Glad to know what you think of me, though. How did you know I was here? Has Ed been in contact?' A glimmer of hope shines in me, lifting me slightly.

'Don't be stupid. Why would I want to talk to Ed?' *Don't mince your words, Gwen!* 'I saw you on the Hive cameras I set up to look after the place while we're waiting for probate. You can never be too careful with an empty property. But as you're staying there I'll disconnect them.' She hesitates. 'Just please be careful.'

Gwen hangs up before I can reply. Which is probably a good thing because I was about to rant about how careful I have been my whole bloody life and I'm not about to start smashing glasses now I'm home. Then I remember the torn dress.

I drop my head into my hands and sigh.

Chapter Ten

'This place smells amazing, Maggie. When I said *wine*, obviously I was hoping for wine and nibbles, but it smells like you've outdone yourself.' Phillip gives me a bear hug as he sniffs intently at the air.

'Thanks, Pip,' I say, enjoying the contact of another human being who is dressed. 'It's just a summer chicken and veg stew but I thought I'd better make something for dragging you both here. Especially on the weekend when I know it's family time.'

I kiss Phillip on the cheek and we follow the rich smell of the stew all the way to the kitchen. The wedding dress has been shoved in the cupboard under the stairs and I have opened the doors to the garden to let in the warmth, and angled the chairs at the table so if everyone sits where I've planned, none of us will have to look at the offending weeds and grass that are taller than I am. Phillip has other ideas.

'Wow,' he says, ignoring my groans and sticking his head out the door into the beautiful sunshine. 'Your garden is *wild*. I mean that in a good way, it's gorgeous. What are you going to do with it?'

'Leave it for Gwen to deal with when she comes to sort out Mum's finances,' I shrug. 'I'm happy to be shot of it all.'

Phillip turns so quickly he catches his ear on the door frame.

'Ouch,' he says, rubbing the sore bit. 'What do you mean, "shot of it"?'

A flurry of noise from the hallway signals the arrival of Perdita. And soon enough she is in the kitchen, delighting at the smell of the food and the sight of her two best friends.

'Maggie was just telling us how she wants shot of these beautiful flowers,' Phillip says, sitting down at the table and taking a large glass of white from my proffered hand.

Perdita raises an eyebrow and looks out into the garden.

'They're weeds, and Gwen can deal with it all.' I sit down opposite Perdita and Phillip who have completely ignored my table plan and are sitting facing the triffids. 'Apparently I can't be trusted not to break stuff anyway. She called to tell me to be careful. That was right after turning off the Hive cameras she put up to protect the house while it's empty. I bet she is more worried about her inheritance now I'm back than she was when the place was empty! I had no idea she'd put them up until she called me last night to tell me to take off Mum's wedding dress, and again this morning to tell me not to steal anything.'

'She's such a princess,' Perdita says, rolling her eyes. 'I hope she definitely has turned them off.'

I nod my head and wave my middle fingers in the general direction of the cameras.

'Princess is not the word I'd use,' adds Phillip. 'Is that why you're here, love? To go through your mum's belongings. Have you come back to get the wedding dress? Did Ed propose after all, or did you have to do it? Is that why you were trying it on, to make sure it fits for your impending nuptials?'

He starts to hum the 'Wedding March' and an ice spike pierces my already very holey heart. In all the shit that's happened since I was last here, I'd forgotten about my hopes of a proposal. I can't tell my friends about the other note I have found, not yet. There's something more important to do first. I shake my head slowly as my bottom lip wobbles all of its own accord. It will be like ripping off a plaster, I am just going to do it.

'Ed's broken up with me,' I blurt.

Saying it out loud to people I know makes it too real. Tears spring out again. Phillip and Perdita are off their chairs and around to my side in an instant. They envelop me in a hug that allows the tears to come more freely, not that I thought that was possible.

'It's just a blip, Maggie,' Perdita says, stroking my hair. At least, I think it is her stroking, it could be either of them. 'He's just having a thirteen-year itch, a worry because you were talking about marriage maybe. Though he's still a shit for putting you through this. Worrying about commitment after all you guys have been through is the worst of the worst.'

'Yeah,' Phillip adds, 'I can only imagine he's just taking some time to remember why you guys got together in the first place and he'll be back with his tail between his legs in no time. Meanwhile you can ride it out here in your inheritance, trying to decide which bits to steal out from under Gwen's nose. I remember when Sam and I had our five-year anniversary − I felt like upping and leaving, too, but we had a kid and a house so I couldn't really.'

I snort a giggle in my haven between their bodies. I know he is only saying that to make me feel better. Phillip and Sam never even argue. But I guess that's what people said about me and Ed before . . . before face-gate.

'It's not a blip,' I say, extracting myself from my friends who are now perched on the table either side of me. 'He's met someone else. Gorgeous Annabelle from his work, with legs up to her chin. He's been seeing her for the best part of a year. I caught them together yesterday . . .' *God, was it really only yesterday?* 'W-when I was sent home from work for an undetermined amount of time because I've been so shit at it lately.'

Perdita starts to say something but I keep going, I need to get all the bad news out before I stop talking.

'And then Ed told me to move out because I'm not on the tenancy of the flat that we've shared together for years. That's why I came to find you yesterday, Perdie. I'm jobless, homeless, pretty much an orphan, and single. Yay me!'

Chapter Eleven

The sun feels like it has risen earlier this morning. I have been up for hours, showered, dressed, breakfasted on leftovers from the meal I'd made for my friends, and am on my third cup of tea from the pot and wondering if I can go back to bed because crying over Ed is easier when I can cocoon myself from the world.

I recheck my phone for the umpteenth time. Still no turgid reply from the shitstorm that is my boyfriend. Or ex-boyfriend, more likely, the longer the silence goes on. I hadn't wanted to admit to the hope that still glimmers in my heart to Perdita and Phillip last night. They turned the air blue after I told them exactly what I'd walked in on and how Ed had dealt with the fallout. So, while we'd eaten the stew – which had been amazing, even if I say so myself – and put the world to as right as we could between us, I had dutifully ignored my phone.

As soon as Phillip had headed back for little Victoria's bedtime, and Perdita had gone to get ready for a hot date with a junior doctor, I had been over to my phone in a shot. Nothing from Ed, just a few messages from Gwen about not making a mess and not ransacking the place with house parties and raves. I couldn't work out if she was being facetious. I almost regretted turning down my friends' offers to cancel their plans so they could stay longer and keep me company. Not that Phillip could cancel Victoria going to bed, but he had been overly keen to get out of having to help.

'It's like she turns into the child of Satan at bedtime, every single night! You'd be doing me a huge favour!'

But instead, I'd turned again to the alcohol cupboard and dragged the soft folds of Mum's wedding dress out from under the stairs to keep me company into the early hours.

'Knock-knock!' A half-arsed wrap of knuckles at the door through the utility room makes me jump.

'Shit,' I hiss, pulling yesterday's cardigan over my shoulders and dragging the wedding dress from the table to hide it underneath.

I know my red, blotchy face looks like a person grieving, and that's OK. But I don't want whoever has just let themselves into my new old house to see the dress that I've been using as a comfort blanket strewn all over the place.

'Is there anyone home?' It's a man's voice, older and not in the least bit akin to one of those home-invasion horror movie types. 'Only I saw some lights on the last few nights and wondered who it could be.'

Great, is nothing sacred in this house?

'I'm in here!' I shout to the bodiless voice, knowing I am being obtuse by not saying exactly where here is. 'Come on in and make yourself at home; oh, you already did,' I add quietly.

A weathered old face pokes itself around the door to the kitchen. The face matches the voice in its lack of serial killer traits. He looks, in fact, like an unkempt Worzel Gummidge, if that was a thing, because Mr Gummidge isn't exactly winning prizes for dapperness himself. I look him up and down as he smiles at me as though I should recognise him.

'Yes?' I say, when it becomes apparent he isn't going to be forthcoming about his identity.

'Can I come in?'

'You are.'

'I suppose I am, aren't I?' He laughs.

I scan the kitchen counters for a weapon to use just in case.

'I'm Pops.' He holds out his hand which looks as if it's made from old leather suitcases that have been left out in the Spanish sun while their owners enjoy one too many pina coladas.

I take it and shake it. It *feels* like an old suitcase, too.

'I'm Maggie,' I say, not quite knowing what else to add. 'My mum used to live here. I used to live here. I guess I do again now.'

Do I? Am I not just staying while my shit of a boyfriend gets his screwing around out of his system and realises he can't live without me? Because I sure don't want to stay here. And I am very sure I want Ed back.

'I know you are, love.' He stares at me for a split second too long. 'You don't remember me, do you?'

I squint at him, slowly shaking my head from side to side.

'No, sorry,' I say. 'Look, it's been a crap few weeks and my brain is all over the place. I'm sure in better circumstances . . .'

I leave the words dangling, hoping Pops will pick them up and manoeuvre them into a semblance of something less awkward.

'Oh, Margaret, you're so like your mother!'

Incredible. Come into my own house and insult me, why don't you?

'Pops. We only met a few times, mind, so maybe I'm not as memorable as you are. I'm the gardener.'

I snort.

'Did you and Mum have an argument or something?' I say, laughing at the state of the gardens.

Pops scratches his grey stubble with the heel of his hand.

'No,' he says. 'Why? Did she say something? I hope she wasn't annoyed with me before she died. I've been coming to tend to the gardens for a while now, so I would have hoped she might have told me if she was annoyed with me.'

His eyebags sag down to his chin and I feel sorry for him.

'No, not at all. I haven't spoken to my mum in months. She never mentioned you.' That seems a bit harsh, given he may very well have been encouraging the weeds to grow for longer than I've been alive. 'I mean, she never mentioned you in a bad way. Or, really, you know. No, I meant . . . the garden. It's . . .'

There is no way of saying it looks like it hasn't been tended for the last thirty years, without just saying it.

'It's a beauty, isn't it? Bit big for me now, though, but your mum always kept me on because she knew how good it was for me to get out of the house. My wife . . . you know. She was a good woman, your mum.'

Pops' rheumy eyes cloud like a White Russian. I want a drink. But not a White Russian. And it is pre-midday. Still not quite appropriate drinking time.

So, Mum did have a conscience hidden beneath the depths of cool exterior, after all. She must have kept Pops on even though he wasn't doing anything at all in the garden because his wife had died and being at home was too full of painful memories. It was a shame she didn't feel the same about having her daughters around the place.

'I haven't got anything to pay you with,' I say, bluntly. Not showing quite the same caring instincts as my mum right now, because my own life is falling apart enough without having to pay for a service that isn't servicing.

'That's OK, I don't need the money. Your mum paid me mostly in gin anyway. But I came around to ask if you would mind if I carried on working? And to see which of you it was who had come back.'

I kick the wedding dress further under the table before I get up and put the kettle on.

'Gwen will be here in a few weeks,' I say, by way of an apology. 'I can't do gin, but I can make you a coffee if you'd like?'

Give the man credit, as soon as the words are out of my mouth, Pops' eyes are on the booze cupboard. I don't budge. I need the alcohol more than he does; he looks pickled enough already.

'I won't stay then.'

There is a small chance that Pops hadn't come to see who was in the house after all, just for some liquid refreshments. I feel he could be my spirit animal right now, were it not for the fact my spirit animal seems to have buggered off with the rest of my life.

'Feel free to carry on doing the garden,' I say. 'I'm not sure how long I'll be here for, though. Or Gwen. Or what we'll be doing with the place now. So, you might need to just check we're here before you start ripping up any weeds.'

Pops shuffles back to the door. I look at him and wonder how he will actually get down to the weeds. Then I remember they are about waist height so shouldn't actually pose a problem.

'That's OK,' he says, leaving the way he came in. 'I've got a key to the garden. And I don't like pulling up weeds, I think it's cruel. I much prefer to talk to the flowers and give them a little water and attention.'

I flick the switch on the kettle and groan into my hands. Two sharp hums signal my phone is vibrating somewhere over by the table.

Ed?

I semi-rush to my phone so as not to look desperate to all the imaginary people judging me – myself.

Can you open the windows in all the rooms to make sure they're properly aired while you're there? Can't have the house becoming stale.

Not Ed after all. As predicted, it's just Gwen, micro-managing me because she thinks I can't cope well enough to air my own stench out of a house. If it wasn't for Gwen, or old, pretend gardeners in the house, I would feel relaxed and quite enjoy the stay away from my London flat. I pull the screen down to refresh it but there are still no new messages from Ed.

What is he doing?

Actually, scrap that. I don't want to think about what he is doing now I am out of the way, especially as he didn't care about having his face stuck in someone else's jacksie when I *was* at home.

I drag the wedding dress back up off the floor, shoving my face into the material and smelling Chanel and something I can't quite place. Probably the recycled rhubarb gin from my stinking breath two nights ago.

'Hello,' a male voice sings through the kitchen.

Oh my God, is there literally not a moment's peace to be had in bloody Norfolk? I thought London was supposed to be the busy one.

'I'm still at the kitchen table,' I shout back, wondering if Pops has already forgotten he has been around to see who is back.

I wipe my face with the back of my hand, seeing yesterday's mascara come away with it. How can so many tears still not wash away Lancôme's finest? I can't be bothered to hide the dress again. Pops won't judge me, lest he wants an earful of how weeds are not friends.

'Hi, I saw that there was someone here last night and I wanted to come and check everything was OK.'

The head that pops around the door this time is not old and grey; it is young and dark and pretty spectacular.

Shit, I think, not for the first time that morning.

'Hi, Nick,' I say, eyeing up the dress on the table and picturing my panda eyes and red nose.

Chapter Twelve

'So then in my haste to get out of it, it ripped a little over my thunder thighs.'

Retelling the story made it seem like I was living some kind of weird Jeremy Kyle-esque reality. *Only living family member finds sibling in dead mum's wedding dress fiasco.* More suited for the pages of the *Daily Star* than the rural outback of Norfolk. Nick is looking at me with an expression I remember well. It makes me want to be fifteen again and hanging out at school before the fear of exams sent us all sprawling away to our rooms to revise. Not that Nick and I ever hung out together, that was only in my head. But it's a look he would subtly bestow on me over a packed classroom for my lack of common sense at least once a week, before he stopped looking at me altogether after Sally Morton's party.

'Gwen was spying on you?' He's moving about the kitchen as though he knows it. I watch as he flicks the kettle on to reboil and takes out two mugs and some coffee. 'No wonder you look so upset.'

'I'm not upset because of Gwen. You must remember what she's like? She hasn't changed – if anything she's got worse with age. Like a fine wine, only the cork popped when she was four and I was born, and she's been festering to the point of vinegary spitefulness ever since. Besides, she's turned the cameras off now so I can forget about her really.'

Nick puts a coffee on the table for me and takes a seat opposite. I no longer care about Pops' gently tended weeds or the mess of toile and lace that I'm hugging close to my body or the fact that I have no idea why Nick has turned up here at my mum's house. I take a sip, careful not to spill the drink over the dress as I bring the mug to my lips. It's milky and sweet, just the way I used to drink it in between classes from a bottle green Thermos flask that I thought was cool but now know to be incredibly pretentious.

He remembers how I like my coffee . . .

'What's got you looking like you've been up all night sobbing over a dead pet then? Because I know your mum has just died and that's sad and all, but you used to call her a worse version of Cruella de Vil.' He drinks his own coffee, relaxing back into the chair as though he belongs here.

And I suppose he does. I was the one who ran away to London at the first opportunity, not Nick Forster. He just stayed and matured into a young man I could stare at all day.

The dress is a sparkly lace-covered elephant in the room that I may as well point out before it becomes too ridiculous to talk about.

'This,' I say, balling it in my hands and lifting it slightly, '*this* is what's made me look like I've been up all night crying. That and the copious amounts of alcohol I've consumed the last couple of nights because my boyfriend has left me and I've had to come back to the arse-end of nowhere to a house that leaves me with a bad taste in my mouth. So, actually, maybe it's all of the above.'

I shrug and scoff ironically. I may as well tell Nick the truth. It's not like he's going to go and spread rumours about me at school, not that he would have done that back then either.

'The idiot boyfriend, who I hope is now an *ex*-boyfriend, is just that, an idiot. And bound to make you cry. Don't mind me if I scoot over that particular part of your life.' *He remembers.* 'But what is going on with the dress? Why were you in it in the first place?'

I hide my face behind the coffee cup. I may have told him I tried the dress on, but I'm not sure I want to tell him *why*.

'I asked Mum if I could borrow her dress for when Ed and I got married.' What the heck, I may as well tell Nick the whole sorry story. 'But she told me she didn't know where it was. I wasn't actually getting married, I just wanted to ask her for when Ed proposed on our anniversary. Turns out he'd rather taste the nether regions of a particularly attractive workmate than spend our anniversary sealing the deal with me. Anyway, I spotted the dress sitting pride of place in my mum's dressing room at her funeral, like a shrine to a marriage that fell to pieces right there amongst her active wear. She lied to me. So I tried it on to spite her.'

'Classic Elizabeth, selfish to the end.'

I mull over Nick's perfectly correct depiction of my mum, biting my tongue to stop myself defending the indefensible just because I am related to her. *Was* related to her.

'I wanted to stick a finger up to her, make her turn in her grave, or whatever the saying is. Only I ended up humiliating *myself* because Gwen saw me and laughed at me and I felt stupid.'

I rummage through the waves of material until I find the rip.

'This is the damage I did – but look what I found sewn into the bodice.'

I hold out the love note, which is so light it flaps about in my fingers despite there being no breeze. Nick takes it carefully and I watch his face as he reads it. He looks just the same as I remember, but with an addition of a sprinkling of grey hairs and some laughter lines that make his once-boyish face look remarkably handsome. I always saw it, the cheeky smile, the twinkling blue eyes, the way he thought about what he was going to say before he said it. But kindness and thoughtfulness were not the top of the boyfriend wish list of a teenager trying desperately to fit in with the cool crowd. Especially when they came hand in hand with a love of reading and spending lunchtimes hiding away in the library to write for the school zine. Nick was a law unto himself, and I wish now that I had allowed myself half the confidence he had.

'I take it *E* is your mum.'

I nod.

'Then *LS* must be your dad?'

I shrug this time.

'I'd know more,' I say, 'if Mum had ever told me anything about him except, "*He isn't around anymore so there's no point in bringing him up.*" Urgh.'

I push the dress off my knee and onto the floor where it sits staring at me like a judgmental child.

'Are there any more notes?' Nick asks. 'What a romantic story.'

'Just one,' I say, shrugging. 'It was pinned to the front of the dress and it says *I love you* in French. No idea what this one says.'

'"Forever yours from this day forward",' Nick says, rubbing his forefinger over the note as gently as if it were a lover.

'Anyway,' I add, ignoring the fire raging in me that Nick can read French. 'Aren't romantic stories supposed to have happy endings? I can't rip up the rest of the dress on the possibility there might be more hidden love letters between my parents who ended up hating each other enough to never see each other again.'

Nick reaches out a hand and places it on my arm. The touch surprises me. I can feel tears spring into my eyes so I jump up out of my seat before they can fall and head over to the sink so I have a reason not to be facing Nick.

'Why not?' he says, ignoring my tears. 'It's not like *you're* going to need it now.'

I grimace at him pointedly and he raises his arms in defence, a glimmer of a grin on his face.

'Sorry!' he adds. 'Not ready for that yet? You're right. Maybe a love story with a sad ending is not what people want. I should know, I work with sad endings every day.'

'What?' I say, turning around from where I had been busying myself rinsing my mug, wondering why the water is running brown and not clear like normal people's taps. 'You're a writer? All those lunchtimes in the library paid off for you then.'

The smile slips from his face, only momentarily but enough for me to notice.

'I'm a solicitor, so I do know how to write, yes. I work in family law. For the good guys, mind. So, the hard work paid off for my career.' The unspoken words between us are written all over Nick's face but he plasters on a smile. 'Are you not just a little bit curious? You could find out more about your dad.'

'I suppose I could.' I reach for the cutlery drawer and drag it open with a squeal of swollen wood against metal. 'Jeez, is there nothing in this place that doesn't need fixing?'

'Two human beings?' Nick asks, eyeing me warily as I pull out a pair of scissors.

'Speak for yourself,' I reply.

I need more than fixing. I need a total reboot. But that will have to wait. For now, Nick has got me thinking about what else might be hidden in the wedding dress that Mum held so close to her heart. I walk back over to pick it up off the tiles and lay it out flat on the table. Nick stands, too, and moves his cup so there's more space. It feels OK, standing here with Nick, about to cut up my mum's old wedding dress. I lift the bodice, trying to find the tear I've already made. That's as good a place as any to start causing more carnage. I hear my phone buzz over by the sink and ignore it; it's only going to be Gwen reminding me what day the bins go out and how to descale the shower like I'm a child. She can bugger right off as far as I'm concerned.

'Right,' I say, lifting the scissors in preparation, 'let's see what we can find.'

I snip away carefully at the edge of the tear, aware that by doing this I will never be able to wear my mum's wedding dress to get married in when Ed changes his mind about his early mid-life crisis and remembers why he fell in love with me in the first place. He'll be back, wanting to make things right and maybe I'll have a fling in the meantime, just to get it out of my system, too, then we'll be evens. I look up at Nick and, catching his eye, my cheeks heat in case he can read my mind. Perdita's words sound in my ears. He is still totally my type.

No! Focus, Maggie.

The dress is tougher than I expected it to be. If scissors can't rip it yet my backside can, what does that say about me? Nothing that's going to help my self-esteem, that's for sure.

'What are you trying to preserve?' Nick asks, nodding to the material bending over the scissors. 'Cut it like you mean it.'

He's right; I don't care about this dress any more than Mum cared about me. I start to hack at it instead, the material making a beautiful ripping sound as the blades shear through it. The skirt comes away from most of the bodice, slithering onto the floor with a thud. Dropping the scissors, I tear at the boning with my fingers. The front of the bodice starts to peel away from the lining and the whalebone – and with a patter like the flutter of butterfly wings, more folded notes drop down onto the table. Nick and I look at each other as my phone buzzes annoyingly from the counter again.

'Oh, bugger off, Gwen!' I say, sticking my fingers up at my phone then swiping the limp fabric onto the floor to be with the rest of the broken dress.

I carefully pick up the notes. Six more, so eight of them in total. And hold them in my hands.

'Maybe you should get that, it might be important.' Nick nods towards my phone which is still buzzing incessantly on the counter.

I put the notes on the table with the one I've already read and step over the material to get to the sink. I pick up my phone, ready to be shouted at by my annoyingly perfect sister and stop abruptly, my heart in my mouth.

'Oh, it's Ed,' I say to the vibrating phone in my hand.

Chapter Thirteen

'Ed? Who's Ed? Is that the ex?'

I can barely hear Nick over the rushing in my ears. The phone is jumping about in my hands and I can't really remember what to do with it. My fingers swipe the phone call, while a part of me is hoping he hangs up before I answer.

'Hello?' I pretend I don't know who it is.

'Mags? It's me, Mags.' Ed's voice sounds just the way it did the first time we shouted to each other over the speakers in Fifth Avenue. The same almost lisp, the same way he rolls the vowels around his mouth like sweets.

You know where else his mouth has been, Mags.

'I'm sorry, who?' I'm being deliberately spiteful, but he deserves to feel at least a little awkward.

'Ed.'

The silence stretches out further than the room. I hold my breath and Nick gives me a look to ask if I'm OK. I turn away from him. I don't want him to see the panic on my face at how unprepared I am.

'Ed, hi,' I answer eventually.

I can hear him scuffling about on the other end of the phone and I wonder where in our house he is poking his toes into the carpet. Maybe the worn grey in the bedroom, or the stained lino in the kitchen, even the threadbare living room carpet that was probably cream when it was laid, back when the house was built, but had turned a deep dirty-coffee colour before we had even moved in.

'Maggie,' Ed starts.

I wait. I'm not going to make this any easier for him. I can feel an apology about to come spouting from his lips. He has never been very good at saying sorry. It always took him an age to decide to say it then it all spewed out so quickly it was hard to make sense of it.

'How are you?'

It's not what I was expecting. But it's a start. He's trying at least.

'I've been better.'

Ed clears his throat and I take the opportunity to sit back down at the table, kicking the dress out of my way as I go. Nick is looking out the door into the garden, but I don't feel that his presence is in the way of my conversation. Which is weird; normally I hate talking on the phone when I have an audience – it makes me self-conscious that what I'm saying is a pile of twaddle.

'Yes, I suppose you have.'

'Was there something you wanted, Ed? Or are you just calling to remind me that I've felt better about myself?'

I see Nick smirk.

What? I mouth at him, a smile edging onto my lips, too.

'No. No, of course not, Maggie. I was just phoning to see how you are, that's all. I've been . . . um . . . kind of missing your voice.'

My stomach feels like lead when I think it should be feeling light as a feather. Ed's missing me.

'Oh.' I kind of huff out the word.

'Look,' Ed says, the scuffing noise in the background getting louder, 'I am feeling bad about what happened.'

'Good.'

'Yes, well, I deserve that.'

'No, Ed, you deserve a lot more than just *feeling bad* but it's a start.'

'I am . . . I am sorry.'

My thoughts all crash together. He has said it. He's sorry.

Nick looks back over at me, his eyebrows creasing together. Without speaking he goes over to the kettle and reboils it yet again, setting our mugs out to refill. I hear him rummaging around in the cupboards as I turn my attention back to my boyfriend.

'I don't know what came over me. I should have talked to you. Made things better between us.'

I nod, somehow knowing that he can sense this over the phone. We always had a sixth sense for that kind of thing.

'You should have, Ed. What you did wasn't fair.'

'I know. I know. It's just hit me, now you're not here, how much I enjoy having you around me, and how I'm not sure I don't want you around me anymore. Maybe when you're more settled at your mum's I can come and visit you?'

YES! I want to shout it from the rooftops.

'Maybe,' I say.

'Maybe,' he replies quietly.

I take a moment to sit quietly once Ed has hung up. I can't think about what has just happened. Not yet. My brain is too buzzing to be able to put the phone call into any kind of order. My eyes are instead drawn to the garden and the knee-high weeds. They may be classed as a nuisance but maybe Pops has a point. They're quite beautiful. Red poppies, blue lavenders, cornflowers, some tall vibrant pink things whose name I have no idea of. They're waving softly in what I imagine to be a nice cool breeze, because the kitchen is now stifling. At least that's how it feels on my pulsing hot face.

'Are you OK?' Nick sets down a fresh coffee in front of me and he's found some biscuits.

I nod. 'They've probably been in the cupboard since I was young. Mum didn't do biscuits, and I certainly didn't bring them with me!'

Nick inspects the packet.

'Yeah, best before January. 1996.'

We both laugh and he offers me the packet anyway. I shake my head vigorously enough to send my hair flying out of its scruffy bun. I pull it loose and let it fall around my shoulders.

'Maggie, are you really OK?'

I don't know if it's the question, or the relief at Ed finally apologising that sets me off. But my bottom lip starts to quake with a life of its own. Nick wraps an arm around my shoulders and squeezes me close to him. He hasn't been this close since that night at Sally Morton's party and it feels good. Comforting, like an old blanket or a favourite sweater. Tears soak into his T-shirt and I'm just glad I cried away most of my mascara last night because the T-shirt looks expensive.

'He called to say sorry,' I sniff.

Nick raises an eyebrow but I ignore him. Ed *had* apologised. He was sorry and he said he was missing me. Coming home had been a good idea after all. If it had only taken Ed two nights to miss me, then things were looking up for our relationship.

'Maybe he was having a thirteen-year wobble.' I try to smile.

'Thirteen years! Wow. I didn't realise. That's a long time to be with someone to just throw it away for a bit of fun.'

I laugh now, remembering again Phillip's summation of Nick's love life.

74

'That must seem like a lifetime for one so promiscuous.'

I can feel his arms tense around me.

'What's that supposed to mean?' he asks me, releasing me from his grip. He looks genuinely affronted.

'Oh, just, you know . . . Phillip said you looked like you have *a way with the ladies,* you know, at Mum's funeral.' I cringe as it comes out of my mouth, but how else can I say man-whore without actually saying man-whore?

'Right, did he now?' Nick says, shaking his head. 'That couldn't be further from the truth. I don't have the time or the inclination, to be honest with you.'

I don't know what to say.

'Are you holding out then?' I ask. 'You've just not found *the one* and you're taking your time looking for her?'

Nick huffs out a little laugh and walks away from me.

'Maybe. Maybe.'

When he turns to face me, his eyes darken. I think back to the party at Sally Morton's house. Unable to face Nick as I had been dragged away, my legs powerless to hold me steady because I had consumed my own body weight in cheap booze. I had wanted to reach out to him then, tell him that I felt the same as he did. But I had been too scared that the girls would mock me and the guys would laugh. It wasn't my fault that I had, and still have, a deep-seated need to be liked by everyone and anyone because validation wasn't forthcoming at home.

How can I still be so embarrassed about what happened? I think.

He's grown into this lusty, Avenger of a body and I'm pretty much still a Raggy Doll. Perdita and I used to laugh about how I would try to make myself look presentable for school without the help of a mum who was very good at hair, or very good at anything maternal, and my bunches would resemble the 80s cartoon rejects. Thank God I never tried to steal her makeup.

'Sorry,' I say, cursing Phillip for telling me made-up stories about Nick. 'It's really none of my business what you get up to. And my friends should mind their own business. I'm sorry. I'm only trying to detract from my own mess of a love life.'

Nick shrugs. 'No need for an apology. But I need you to know it's not true, never has been. Are we going to read the other notes you found?'

His shoulders look tense, raised up around his ears, but he shakes them out and raises his arms to the sky, lifting his T-shirt so I catch a glimpse of his belly button. It's surrounded by a scattering of hair and I can't draw my eyes away from the line the hair takes down to the waistband of his jeans. My face heats even more than I thought possible as I try to clear my head. The room feels as if it's shrunk to the size of my pea-shaped brain.

'If it's OK,' I say, feeling Nick's eyes on me as my own drop to the floor, 'I'm just going to put them away to look at when I'm feeling less emotional.'

Nick chews his cheek. 'Sure. I'd better head off, I've got work to do. Do you want me to put this upstairs out of your way?' He nods at the decimated wedding dress on the floor.

'If you wouldn't mind,' I say, sad that he's leaving and confused that I'm sad. 'Nick, thank you for coming over.'

'Anytime, Mags. It's nice to have you back in Haverley.'

He scoops the dress up in his arms and waddles to the kitchen door, quite unaware of how his familiar name calling has hit me right in the solar plexus.

'Temporarily, Nick. Temporarily,' I whisper back.

Chapter Fourteen

'So he's a sad dad then, only he's not a dad.'

Perdita has hold of one end of a rusty pipe and Phillip has the other. I'm in the middle with the gaffer tape and some scissors.

'What?' I huff out the question as I lean between the lifted floorboards in the bathroom and try to do the best I can with my layman's tools.

Gaffer tape solves everything, Perdita had told me when I called in another emergency with my best friends. A leaky pipe in one of the bathrooms was turning the ceiling in the living room a nice shade of green and it was only a few drops away from spilling down onto the already stained carpet when I got into the shower this morning and heard it tap-tap-tapping under the floor.

'A sad dad,' Perdita answers, sweat gathering on her pristine brow. 'What the fuck, can I let go now? My arms are literally going to fall off.'

'Literally not going to fall off, Perds,' Phillip tries to add whilst being unable to breathe with the angle his head's at. 'Figuratively, maybe.'

'Your arms will *literally* be ripped out of their sockets if you don't shut up,' Perdita swears under her breath and tries to kick Phillip but luckily I'm in the way and she ends up poking me in the thigh with a remarkably sharp toe.

'Ow! Guys, stop,' I say, lifting my head out of the floorboards and glancing either side of me.

It would be hilarious if it wasn't for the fact it was only one of a list of a million things that need fixing in the house. Almost as though Mum treated the rotten wood and the rusty pipes the same way Pops treats the weeds. I tear the last of the tape with my teeth and let my friends know it's safe to release the pipe gently. I kneel up to turn the taps on, the whole house judders and groans and we hold our breath, waiting for another gush of water from the slimy green section of the pipe I've just covered over with the kidnapper's favourite tool. But the water flows out of the pipe and nowhere else, much to my relief. And probably my friends', too, seeing as they look like a pair of sweaty tomatoes.

'Drink?' I ask, chipper now.

'Gin,' Phillip answers, though the hour hand is not yet past midday. Nobody argues with him.

I'd gone to bed last night thinking about Nick and Ed in equal measure. My relationship looks like it might not be doomed after all and I am happy about that. But I am confused over the short interlude I'd had with Nick and how it had ended so abruptly. I don't even know why Nick came over, not really. He said he had seen the house wasn't empty anymore and wanted to check, just like Pops had, and he'd seemed at home here. But it has been more than seventeen years since we last spoke to each other and I can't help but wonder why he had *really* come over. So I'd asked my friends for advice.

'A sad dad,' Perdita sips her drink, the ice cubes clinking in the glass, 'is a single dad who is on the hunt for a new girlfriend. He can sniff out the desperate – not saying you're desperate by the way, Mags – and homes in on them, showering them with *I can't believe it!* and *he's such an idiot not being able to see what he's thrown away.* Then, when the unsuspecting woman is feeling just happy enough with the compliments he swoops in with his dick and bob's your uncle. For five minutes. Then he buggers off again, contented, leaving behind a mortally wounded heart that was already a broken and empty shell. A sad dad.'

Phillip makes a noise that could be an agreement, or it could just be a reaction to the amount of gin I put in his glass beneath the splash of orange.

'How is this a thing? And how do I not know about it? Also, Perds, isn't that a little judgemental?'

'Phillip, when you're as permanently single as I am, you become learned in the pursuits of the man who is only after one thing.'

We're sitting outside now, amongst Pops' weed friends. The warm August air is hugging us and bringing with it the sweet scent of the garden and the buzz of the bees. I relax into my deckchair, knowing that getting out is going to be too hard anyway. I'd told Perdita and Phillip about Nick's visit over our WhatsApp group last night and Perdita has been rooting around in her grab bag of anecdotes to work out why.

'So, you think he came over to get into my knickers?' I take a sip and think about how kind Nick was being, making me coffee and bringing me decades' old biscuits.

'He does have the reputation,' Perdita shrugs.

'No, he doesn't – that was made up by Phillip! He's a good guy, he came over to check on the house,' I say, thinking how comfortable my time with Nick had been.

'So, you're telling me you haven't had any sad dad texts since Ed decided to taste test his workmates?' Perdita asks.

I am struck with a pang of what feels like dread.

'Here was me thinking Alan really did want to show me his Subbuteo set,' I reply.

'Who's Alan?'

'One of Ed's football friends.' My stomach sinks.

'And when did he message you?'

'When I was on the train to Norfolk, ewwww. Oh, ewwww.'

'Point in case and no judgement from me, Phillip, just a good sense of what's what when it comes to men.'

I sip my drink, feeling a foot shorter.

'Well, I can vouch, as a person with a penis, that not all men are like that.' Phillip raises his glass in a toast.

We join him and clink silently in mid-air as none of us can get out of our deckchairs to actually reach each other. Perdita gives me the side-eye.

'You could have a go, though, Maggie, now you're single,' she says, sipping her drink all innocently. 'I mean, he *is* bloody gorgeous. Just protect yourself and go wild.'

Phillip is nodding. 'If I was single and that way inclined, I would.'

'Thanks for the suggestion, guys, but . . .' I stop, *do I want to tell them about Ed getting in contact*? 'I'm just going to take my time away from the opposite sex for the moment.'

'That's a good idea, love,' Perdita says.

'Perds can make up for your drought with the number of men she's sleeping with,' Phillip adds, winking at Perdita.

She dips her fingers in her glass and sprays him with drink.

'OK, so how many people have you got it on with recently?' Phillip asks.

I don't join in this conversation, I just listen quietly in the background, turning over the idea of Nick in my head. I think about the love notes tucked away between cookery books in the kitchen. I put them there for safe keeping, including the one I found at Mum's funeral, and I haven't looked back at them in the few days they've been keeping Delia and The Hairy Bikers company. I don't want to bring them up now because the two Ps will want me to go and get them so they can psychoanalyse the shit out of them and come to the conclusion I came to years ago: that my parents are the root of all my problems.

My heart feels like a heavy weight, knowing that my dad could write letters of love to my mum who had a blackened soul, yet he didn't have the time to want to get to know me. Or Gwen. But her soul had dropped not far from the apple tree and, given the multitude of angry texts she's sent me since I arrived at the house, her apples are rotten to the core. What was it about me that made him run a mile? Because he didn't when Gwen arrived. She may have only been four when he left but she has memories of him which she reminds me of every so often because it boosts her superiority. But me? Nothing. Not even a pretend memory that I can dip into now and again because he vanished before I was even flung into the world. Is he still trying to forget me? Is he OK with the fact that he has a child he has never even seen, and one he abandoned when she was a toddler? Or is he out there somewhere, trying desperately to find me and failing hideously because I am now in the same place I was when I was born? Not hard to find.

'What do you think?' Phillip taps me on the shoulder with his cold glass, making me jump. A cool trickle of condensation drips down to my elbow and drops onto a thistle.

'Sorry, what?' I ask, flushing.

'Are you OK, Maggie?' Perdita adds. 'Only, you look like you've been away with the fairies for the last ten minutes. Though, given our surroundings, it's not at all surprising.'

She nods at the weeds that we literally had to bash down with our chairs to make a space to sit. I laugh and turn my attention back to my friends. They've saved me on more than one occasion and I owe them my ears.

'Yeah, I'm OK; I'm just thinking about how much work there is to do on the house before we sell it. You'll never guess who else turned up today?' I say, planting a smile on my face ready to tell them about Pops, world's worst gardener who my mum took pity on because of his dead wife.

Perdita springs as upright as she can in her deckchair which is already in relaxing mode at the lowest setting. Her arms flail about, trying to find purchase.

'What?' she yells. 'There is no way you can sell the house! We grew up here. We have so many memories here. Phillip, tell her.'

She splutters out a few more words that I can't decipher and I look to Phillip for some backup. Wrong. He's looking as apoplectic as Perdita is.

'Guys!' I say. 'You may have nothing but wonderful memories of this place, but it wasn't exactly an Enid Blyton novel for me growing up here, was it?'

Phillip cocks his head to the side. 'Well yes, it was actually.'

'I'd normally punch a guy about to mansplain but I'm giving Phillip the benefit of the doubt here,' Perdita says, blowing him a kiss.

Phillip raises an eyebrow at her and carries on.

'There were no parents in Enid Blyton books, the kids were left to fend for themselves with lashings of ginger beer and tongue sandwiches to last them a week, and they experienced amazing adventures *every* bloody school holiday and didn't ever get rickets. That was us, Mags, only we had stolen vodka and Walkers crisps.'

I deflate into my seat.

'OK, so wrong analogy. What I mean is, that the bad memories here outweigh the good for me. Why would I want to keep it? I'll be heading back to London soon anyway; I have a job and a life there. And Gwen won't leave her high-flying job to take over at Chez Moneypit Hellhole. She's far too important for that.'

'But—' Phillip starts, and I hold up my hand to stop him.

'No buts, I can't stay here,' I say, my throat filled with cotton wool at the thought of selling my childhood home. 'I just can't.'

Chapter Fifteen

Pops holds up a watering can from between the sea of weeds as I plod into the kitchen this morning. I jump pretty much through the roof and back up to my bed when I catch sight of him in the garden. It's a godforsaken early time to be watering weeds, but I can't be seen as ungrateful so once my heart has recovered, I offer him a little wave and lift the kettle back up at him. He nods. Then a second thought must occur to him as he points towards the booze cupboard.

I shake my head and fill the kettle. This morning I have decided to get up early, make proper coffee and start to make headway through some of Mum's old paperwork. Gwen's annoying daily texts have dwindled and she now sends me the occasional reminder that I am useless and should leave *her* stuff alone. But maybe I can show her just how *useless* I'm not. There are piles of random paperwork dotted all over the house. At least if I can organise it into sensible piles then it will be easier to sort through.

I reach for the coffee, my hand darting past the cookbooks on the shelf below, and the love notes that I still haven't dared to look through. I take Pops' mug and a Jaffa Cake out into the garden, looking apologetically at the three flattened patches of weeds my friends and I made for the deckchairs.

'Here you go,' I say, handing him his coffee. He takes it in both thick, tanned, arthritic hands, a twinkle in his eye. 'Don't get too excited, it's just coffee.'

'Nothing Irish or German or French about it, then?' He looks down at the drink as though I'd laced it with poison.

'I didn't know alcoholic coffee came in so many different varieties,' I say, sipping my own virgin coffee, which to my taste buds seems perfect. 'How about we make it to 9 a.m. before we start thinking about drowning out our woes?'

He gives me a weak smile.

'Sorry about the flattened bit, but my friends and I sat out here yesterday. It was such gorgeous weather and the house smelt like rust because we'd been fixing an old leak that my mum must have left, along with so many other . . .' I stop talking. Pops doesn't care if we were fixing pipes or having a mass orgy, he's just here for the plants and to get away from the memories of his dead wife. 'Anyway, I'll leave you to get on with your watering before the sun comes up properly and it just evaporates away.'

Pops grunts at me and I turn back to the house and the enormity of the task ahead of me.

'Thank you, young lady,' Pops barks as I shut the kitchen doors.

I smile to myself. He may have the exterior of an old gnarly oak tree but I'm sure that deep down he's all heart. He won't kill anything in the garden, so he must have a conscience of some sort or another.

My phone pings in the back pocket of my dungaree shorts. Nick.

Have you read any more of the notes yet? Fancy a road trip with me today? I could use a female opinion?

No and yes (intriguing, can you not ask your mum?)

When we were at school, I'd heard that Nick's mum was one of those mums who welcomed anyone into her home. Nick didn't have a lot of friends growing up, just a few really good ones. Looking back, I don't blame him, most of the boys in our year were single-minded, monosyllable-grunting, chest-pounding, self-proclaimed ladies' men. But then they were the magnetic core of the social circle at school. If you weren't *with* them, you were floating around in the black hole that was social pariahism and that was the nightmare of every high school student ever. Except Nick.

So, whenever Nick had taken friends home to his beautiful semi-detached suburban family house, I imagined his mum had scooped them up on the driveway and cuddled them in through the front door. I had been over to his house only the once, but the smell of freshly baked scones and newly picked irises had stayed with me for ever. I can still picture the floral three-piece suite in the living room, littered with books and newspapers that looked well-read and not just for show, the kitchen piled with baked goods and not empty alcohol bottles. The whole house oozed comforting love and I hadn't wanted to leave. But I had only been there to deliver some homework that Nick had dropped in the playground when he'd been rugby tackled to the floor for ignoring Brian White's call to kick his ball back. Nick's head had been stuck in *The Hobbit*, so he hadn't seen the ball or heard Brian's yells because he was in a faraway land featuring small people with hairy feet. But Brian had thought he was just being rude; either that or he wanted someone to show off his new tackling techniques on and Nick was a viable option.

I had tiptoed in the door when Mrs Forster had opened it, nervously looking around, not quite believing that family homes could be so cosy. But I'd run off without so much as a hello at Nick, because seeing him out of his uniform was a step too far for my teenage nerves.

I smile at the memory and wave at Pops as I head out of the kitchen and through to the cluttered office at the front of the house, bashing out an email to work to ask about my return date as I go. It is the best place to start, seeing as the paperwork in here is almost as high as the room itself. The dusty windows look out over the weed-covered shingle drive and I was so lost in my work that I didn't see the battered Volvo pull up a few hours later. Not until Nick rang the doorbell.

'So,' I say, clicking my belt on, 'where are we heading and what's the big secret?'

Nick laughs and throws his arm over my seat to reverse back out onto the quiet country lane.

'No secret,' he says, his tongue between his teeth as he concentrates, 'I just couldn't be bothered to type it all out in a message when I knew I'd be with you in a few hours. If there's one thing you need to know about me, Maggie, it's that I'm not a massive social communicator. No social media, very few texts.'

'Oh,' I say, looking at Nick's tanned arms as he changes gear and heads in the direction of the coast. 'Fair enough. So will you tell me where we are going now? I like a road trip as much as the next person, but I'd like to know how long I'll be away so I can plan things like toilet stops and food and drink and—'

I stop when I see the corner of Nick's mouth twitch.

'I thought it was your sister who was the anally retentive organiser!' he jokes.

Obviously Gwen leaves a mark wherever she goes.

'We're not going far,' he says, when he sees my raised eyebrow. 'No toilet stops needed, probably. Though there is a toilet where we are going. And I've packed some snacks.'

He nods to the back seat and a waiting green and white M&S bag.

'Nice.'

'Don't get your hopes up. It's not me who shops in Marks'.'

Who is it then? Wife? One of the girlfriends?

He is a man of mystery, is Nick. I resist sneaking a peek at the snacks to avoid being disappointed by Asda Smart Price chips and dips masquerading in a Marks' bag.

'So, tell me where we're going then.'

Nick winds down his window and I do the same. It's the first week of September and the air is thick with the dust left behind from the combine harvesters. It whips through the car, sending my hair flapping all over the place. I reach up and tuck it into the neck of my T-shirt.

'It's my mum's sixtieth birthday next month and my dad hasn't been very well this year, so he's asked me to take over the organisation of the party. Hey, maybe I enlisted the wrong sister for help.'

I punch him gently on the arm, surprised at how bouncy his bicep is. I swallow and turn back to the road.

'What is there left to do?' I ask, watching the fields pass us by, seagulls swooping behind the tractors as they plough over the newly shorn crops.

I'm thinking he's taking me present shopping, or to pick out the wine. That would be a nice way to spend the afternoon after a morning bent over decades-old credit card bills and Tesco Clubcard vouchers. Nick sighs.

'Well, there's the venue to double-check and pay the balance on. The food to organise. Some kind of entertainment to book. Oh, and decorations.'

'Did your dad sort anything at all?' I ask, laughing.

'He, um . . .' Nick clears his throat. 'He paid the deposit on the barn we're going to see and sent out invites last year.'

The car falls silent and I hope I haven't put my foot in it.

'He was diagnosed with vascular dementia in January and it's all been a bit difficult. Mum and I knew something was wrong because he'd do things that just weren't him, you know? He'd forget what time of day it was or take an age to remember the word for something he used every day. It progressed faster than we all thought it would. He's just one big bag of confused limbs now and it's getting harder every day. Mum isn't sure how much longer he has left.'

Nick clears his throat again and stares at the road ahead, the sea becoming visible in the distance over the gently undulating hills.

'I'm so sorry, Nick,' I say, placing my hand gently on his forearm. 'Dementia is such a cruel disease.'

'Thank you, Maggie,' he says, breaking the almost awkward silence and smiling at me. 'I know this all seems a bit weird, seeing as we hadn't really seen each other in over fifteen years up until a few weeks ago. I feel a bit like I've just invaded your time back at home and I didn't mean to. I really only dropped in to check on the house. But it's good to be with you again.'

I feel a blush rising in my cheeks, glad of the road to keep Nick's eyes from me. He doesn't seem like a *sad dad* or someone who is trying to get me back for a high school rejection. And it has been good spending time with him in the short space we've had since I've been back. But my intuition when it comes to the opposite sex is completely off-kilter at the moment, so Nick could be trying to get into my knickers right now and I'd be none the wiser.

There are worse ideas. I shrug, stretching my legs out into the footwell of the Volvo.

'I'd be happy to help you, Nick, if you'd do me the honour of helping me with something in return?' I ask quietly, thinking about the pile of French love letters in the front pocket of my dungarees.

'Anything,' he replies.

So I draw them out and flatten them on my knees.

Chapter Sixteen

'Que ton amour soit pour toujours dans mon cœur,' I say in stilted French, reading out the letter with the earliest date, the two already translated tucked carefully back in my pocket.

We sit in silence. The thump, thump, thumping of the tyres on tarmac a gentle background noise.

'Even with your French accent, it sounds so romantic,' Nick says eventually, breaking the wordless pause. I ignore his jibe. 'What a lovely thing to write – do you know what it says?'

'Nope. Like I said, my French is practically non-existent. And all the notes are written in French, so apart from *I love you,* the notes are all Greek to me . . . or French.'

'May your love be forever in my heart,' Nick says, and I feel a small flutter of wings in my stomach.

'Pardon?'

'That's what the note says, *may your love be forever in my heart,* or nearabouts anyway,' Nick says, and the butterflies flit out of the open window. 'What do you think happened?'

'Me.'

Nick casts his eyes in my direction but I don't return the contact. He shifts gears and indicates to turn into an even smaller country lane where the grass verges seep onto the road and attack from both sides with long spindly fingers of soft wild wheat.

'My dad left before I was born,' I remind him, as an explanation of sorts. 'He didn't leave when Gwen came along, just me. Like I said the other day, she tells me routinely how much she remembers him. She was only four so I doubt she remembers him at all – I mean, I can barely remember what I had for breakfast.'

The joke isn't even that funny, but the laughter is what we both need to lift the air. Nick pulls the car up a dirt and gravel drive and parks in front of an old barn with traditional Norfolk flint and red bricks which are somehow managing to hold themselves up despite their jaunty angle. He switches off the ignition and the engine ticks over as it cools.

'Maggie.' His dark brown eyes are searching my face, jet-black lashes flickering. 'Your dad didn't leave because of you. He never got to meet you; how could it be your fault? I'm sure if he had had the chance to meet you, he would have loved you. How could he not?'

Ed used to say the same thing to me, every time Gwen would boast about her memories of the man who had shared our genes. *It's not you, Maggie. It's probably your lush of a mother.* And like a shower of emotion, I wish Ed were here with me now, gathering me up in a bear hug and whispering in my ear that we would get through this together, just like he always used to. *It's me and you against the world, Mags.*

'Thanks, Nick,' I say, swallowing down the cotton wool of emotion lodged in my throat. 'Shall we go in?'

'Maggie,' he says, his hand now on the door handle, 'I meant what I said about helping you find your dad, if you want me to? I speak French, properly! Let me take the letters; I can translate them for you and then we'll have a bit more to go on. We've already got initials, places, dates. There are so many ways to search for people these days and, to be honest with you, it would be a nice distraction from what's going on in my life to help you with what's going on in yours.'

'A party for a papa?' I really need to stop making awful jokes.

Nick snorts kindly and removes his hands from the door handle.

'Let's start with the party, shall we? Then I'll look at your letters tonight.'

'OK, but I can't let you take the letters, they're all I have of my dad. How about you photograph them instead, would that work? Just don't go posting them on social media.'

Nick raises an eyebrow.

'For starters, there's no way I'd post something like this on social media, and I've already told you I don't even have a social media presence. I'm not the most social offline and I don't need another platform to advertise that fact. Photos it is.'

He takes the letters out of my hands and I give him the two from my pocket. As he carefully takes pictures with his phone, I stretch up out of the car and roll my head around on my neck as though we've been driving for longer than the forty-five minutes it has taken us to get to the north Norfolk coastline and this rickety old barn in the middle of a grassy field. Nick joins me moments later and I put the letters carefully back in the front pocket of my dungarees. The sea is just visible over the drop of the gentle hill the barn is perched upon, but because of the clouds that have dropped from the sky and are currently sitting pretty in the air all around us, we have to squint to see where the clouds end and the sea begins.

'I see the sea first!' we both yell at the same time, our heads turning to each other, and this time we really do laugh.

'Your family used to do that, too?' Nick asks me.

I'm still laughing but I shake my head, my ribs aching.

'No, Phillip and Perdita and I do it now on our yearly trip to the seaside. Winner gets fish and chips from the other two. We have been known to say it all the way back in Haverley to get out of having to pay!'

As we walk together towards the barn, Nick points his keys towards the Volvo and presses a button. The car beeps locked.

'I thought your car was too old for central locking.'

'Hey, it may look like diarrhoea, but that trusty steed has done me well for longer than my mum's brand-new KA did her.'

'True, and at least you have a car!'

The nearer we get to the barn, the more I can see of the interior through the floor-to-ceiling windows down one side.

'I don't suppose you have much need for one living in London,' he adds.

'No.'

I'm distracted from thinking about going back to London by the newfound love I am feeling for this wonky old building. Through the window I can see the beams look like they've done a few rounds with the termites and lost. Pitted with holes and flaking away at the edges, their rough beauty fits perfectly with the leaning walls and modern glasswork.

'This place is amazing.'

My face is squished against the window to try and get a better view.

'It is, isn't it?' Nick is beside me, his own hand shielding the glass from the glare of the sun. 'We could go inside instead of smudging the windows; I'm not sure we're covered for the added expense of a window cleaner.'

He holds up a key and the corner of his lips lift.

Inside the barn is even more perfect. The red-brick floor is worn through decades of use, the walls much the same. I run my fingers along the back wall, loving the smoothness of the flint, dotted with razor sharp points that could cause damage to any drunken members of the upcoming party who inadvertently fall against them. At the far end is a small bar, equipped with sink and fridge and the remnants of the last bash looking out from behind the glass door in the form of a bottle of fizz with its foil jagged around a rubber stopper.

'Your dad did a good job when he found this place. I can just imagine it lit up with a million fairy lights along the back wall, reflected in the window; tables with freshly picked wildflower bunches and candles in jars. I can picture your mum in a flower headdress like a giant daisy chain or a . . .'

I stop talking because in all my excitement of picturing the barn how I would love to see it, I realise I have no idea if Nick's mum even likes flowers or if she gets bouts of hay fever that would mean she'd look like she was crying through her whole party if I cover the place in floral displays. Nick is staring at me, his face giving nothing away.

'Sorry,' I say, digging the toe of my ballet flat into a worn dip in the brick.

'No, no, that's perfect. That's exactly why you're here.' He is still watching me, and for a beat I watch him back.

I snort, too embarrassed to not fill the silence. 'See, my skills are almost as good as Gwen's!'

'Yes, but you come without the attitude,' he says, nudging me with his shoulder, his eyes twinkling. 'I really like the idea of the fairy lights along here.'

He points at the far wall and studies it harder than might be normal. We're both looking at it as the sun appears to burn off the clouds and spread its warmth through the glass and onto the flint. We raise our eyebrows at each other and turn. The sea is now glistening and sparkly, the windows perfectly aligned to watch the tips of the water flicker white. A line of trees on either side direct our gaze to the water unnecessarily, as that is all I can think about looking at right then. It's beautiful. Truly beautiful. Our jaws hit the floor.

'This is really perfect,' Nick says, and I have to agree. But I'm not picturing it for a birthday party, I'm picturing Ed and me holding hands in front of this giant window, our friends looking on at us as we promise each other eternal love and companionship. Me in a new wedding dress that isn't massacred by scissors, Ed in a bow tie.

I take out my phone and start clicking the camera at the views and the interior.

'Great idea,' Nick says to me, still staring out at the sea. 'We can use photographs to plan where the tables with freshly picked wildflowers and candles in jars will go. Oh, here, I forgot to give you this.'

He reaches into his pockets and hands me a small bag of pistachios.

He remembers.

I take them and thank him warily, remembering how I used to always have a bag of these with me at school to pick on throughout the day. People used to moan at me for the crispy bits of inner shell I would leave on the desk because they were paper thin and impossible to clear up without a vacuum cleaner.

'And the loos are through the door to the side of the bar.'

'Road trip essentials,' I say, smiling. 'You're the best.'

We look at each other again for a moment longer than necessary.

'So, where do we get enough bunches of flowers to decorate, say, nine large circular tables without it costing me my spare kidney?'

I turn my back to the window and sit down cross-legged on the floor to lean against it, so I can crack open the pack of nuts and dive in.

'You said you were a family solicitor – surely you could drape the flowers in gold leaf and still have spare change for the bottles of Cristal?'

'Actually, Margaret, I think you'll find I do a lot of work pro bono,' he answers, his eyes twinkling some more. 'My interests are to do with people fleeing domestic violence, mostly women but not always, and they have limited funds because manipulative money games is one of the ways they have been abused. So, my cash flow isn't all it could be cracked up to be.'

The smile drops from his face. 'Plus, the extra care we need for my dad is costly.' He claps his hands to shake himself out of his reverie. 'So that's why we need to do *this* as cheaply and cheerfully as possible.'

'Well, you can count on me to help with that. Having never been a great one with savings, I know how to spot a bargain when I see one. In fact, I know just where to start.'

Chapter Seventeen

'So he's gorgeous *and* he has a good heart, phew.' Perdita fans her face.

The three of us are hanging out at her Airbnb apartment this evening and I have been regaling them with how amazing my afternoon was. I hadn't been able to help myself talk about Nick, the way he's caring for his mum and dad, the barn, the electricity that had turned the air static. OK, maybe that last bit I'd kept to myself, but the rest was fair game.

The Airbnb flat is in the centre of the city, overlooking the river and the nightlife that is happening on the opposite bank. I can practically feel the bass from the clubs and pubs lining the water beating a rhythm in my chest. Ten years younger and I would have been marshalling my friends over there. Now I'm happy to nurse a large glass of wine and some baked Camembert that Perdita was given as a thank you gift from one of her clients. *He knew me well, what can I say?* she'd answered my questioning look.

Phillip lounges back on the recliner, looking as though he's about to take part in a counselling session. I've got my parents' love notes still tucked into the front pocket of my dungarees and my hand itches over the top of them.

'Ed's been in contact,' I say, dropping my hand and deciding on the more urgent of the two things on my mind. 'He messaged to say sorry and he'd had a huge bout of cold feet and commitment panic. And we've been sort of texting each other again. I think the space has done both of us some good.'

'Oh, I knew you two would see sense.' Perdita claps her hands together and spills her wine in the process, mopping it up unsuccessfully with her free hand.

'He was the one dicking about, Perds,' Phillip pipes up from his thinking chair. 'Maggie didn't need to see sense. She just needed not to see naked people stuck to her boyfriend's face.'

'Yes, thank you, love.' I blow him a kiss. 'But I know what you mean, Perdita. It takes two people to fail in a relationship of two people. I'm just glad he's apologised and the communication channels are open again. You never know, maybe the trip to the barn today was a sign of things to come, and not just for Nick's mum.'

'What? Do I need to go hat shopping?' she says, humming the 'Wedding March'.

My brain turns to Nick and I gloss over the moment in the barn, because it wasn't a *moment* moment, it was just the sun coming out and brightening the day, that was all. I look coyly into my glass and imagine myself walking down the centre of the barn, through an aisle of chairs wrapped in taffeta bows, towards a man who is dressed in a morning suit of rich navy. I'm almost certain it's Ed waiting for me near the windows . . . yet there is something comfortingly unfamiliar about the broad shoulders that can't possibly belong to my boyfriend.

'Oh, Maggie, look at you, all goo-goo eyes! Here, let me get you some more wine.' Perdita continues humming the 'Wedding March', using my leg to push herself up from the sofa to go and refill our glasses and top up the crudités.

'Has anyone else got any gossip? I don't want to hog the evening with *my* life,' I ask, holding my glass up for Perdita to throw another glug of wine into it.

'Victoria decided to shove a piece of Lego up her nose this morning,' Phillip says. 'That's about the extent of my life at the moment. It's nice having something fun to talk about that doesn't involve a small child. As much as I love her with all my heart, she's like a black hole for conversations. It's also really nice to have you guys home, even if it's just for a short while.'

'Yes, it's just like old times but with more money and better dress sense,' Perdita adds.

'Speak for yourself,' I say to Perdita as she laughs at her joke.

The room lulls into a comfortable silence, punctured sporadically by Phillip breaking celery with his teeth.

'So,' I blurt, unable to hold it in any longer, 'do you remember the love note I found pinned to Mum's old wedding dress at her funeral? Well, I found a load more and Nick is going to help me decipher them and try to track down the sender who we think might be my dad.'

'What?' Perdita and Phillip both bolt upright.

'Maggie, that's HUGE news!' Perdita chokes out over her wine that had gone down the wrong way. 'HUGE. This should definitely have come before Ed.' Then she looks at me kindly and adds, 'Although, it shows how happy you are about being back in touch with him and I'm glad. But, more about your *dad*, please.'

I'm not sure where to start. I knew that my friends would be excited but deep down I also know they're going to be massively disappointed in what I've got so far. The idea that my dad could be out there, waiting for me to find him, *is* massively exciting though, and the tumble dryer in my stomach is more than reminding me of that.

'His initials are LS,' I say, my limbs shaking with the thrill of it all, and I tuck my feet up under me and get ready to tell them all that I know. 'He can speak perfect French as they're all written in French. There's no mention of Gwen so far, so they must be from before she was born.'

'Rose from the burning gates of hell, more like,' Phillip pipes up.

I laugh a little inside but ignore him as I don't want this exciting news to be centred around Gwen and for the mood to drop, as it inevitably does when she's mentioned. Instead, I pull the letters from my pocket.

'He starts off with "I love you" and something about being forever in his heart,' I say, looking at the pile of letters in my hand and flicking between the three I understand. Perdita looks dreamy-eyed, and Phillip looks sceptical. 'And Nick's going to translate the rest and let me know what they say.'

'Fun times ahead for you two, then,' Phillip says, winking.

Perdita throws a slice of red pepper at him to shut him up and he catches it in his mouth. We are all so momentarily stunned, the room falls silent as he crunches on his winnings.

'Oh, and I found the letters sewn into my mum's wedding dress which is *so* romantic. And it proves my mum hasn't always had a stone-cold heart of pure white ice, surely? It just frosted over when she fell pregnant with me.'

'Oh my God, that's just so romantic!' Perdita is staring into the distance over her wine glass. 'What do you think your dad was called? Larry? Lincoln, Leonardo, Levi?'

The same question has been going around and around in my head since I read the first letter. But I don't have a clue. That's the thing. There are no clues about him at all in my life. No middle names given to Gwen or me that could be constructed from a male L, no passwords written down anywhere. No great hulking file of papers with his name written on them and the mystery revealed within it. Nothing. These letters are all I have.

'So Nick is helping you find him, how?' Phillip asks, holding his hands out for the letters.

Phillip is one of my best friends, but just as I didn't want to let the letters go to Nick, I can't bring myself to hand over the only piece of my dad that I have left to Phillip and his pizza hands.

'I can let you look at them from here,' I say, holding them up one by one as Phillip casts his eyes over them. 'Nick is a family solicitor, apparently, he has access to . . . information that I might not.'

'A family solicitor? Wow, he has done well, hasn't he? Kind, jawline of Superman, clever and ethical – is there anything the man can't do?' Phillip laughs. 'But those letters are lovely, Mags. You've got his handwriting.'

I look again at the love notes and notice, for the first time, that my dad loops his y's the same way I do. His long, sloping letters look just like mine, only slightly drunk on the page. Tears prick at my eyes and my lip wobbles. This paper has my genes entwined throughout it and I am going to find the man who wrote them if it is the last thing I do. And it very well might be, as I am so drunk now I could fall asleep forever – or throw up. I work out which one it is going to be a moment too late.

Chapter Eighteen

My phone wakes me. A caterwauling of noises thrumming into my skull which already feels like it is hosting an illegal rave. It's Ed. I grunt into it, only realising a moment too late that he's video calling me and now has a great view of the side of my face.

'Good morning, Mags,' he says, his voice tinny. 'Maggie, where are you? That's not your mum's house. Your house.'

I look around. He's right. And particularly astute when he wants to be. Rubbing the sleep out of my eyes and pushing back the hair that's stuck to my face with dribble with my free hand, I switch the call to audio only. On a scale of one to I'd-like-my-girlfriend-back, I'm near the bottom if not below it at the moment.

'I stayed with Perdita last night,' I say, gagging at the smell of my own breath.

'You're in London?' His voice sounds excited.

'No. Not at *her* flat – that's full of naked Scandinavians – she's in Norfolk working her magic on Delia, allegedly. She's in an Airbnb.'

Ed laughs. I've missed his laugh. It's gravelly and makes him sound like a smoker, which he's not because that's bad for him, and he doesn't do things that are bad for his health. I roll over in bed and imagine he's next to me. We've been out dancing and fallen asleep fully clothed with our limbs entwined and our mouths working their magic long after our brains have fallen over the edge. We'd snuggle up together and have sleepy, hungover sex and then Ed would get up and make us tea and a full English.

'I was just calling to see how you are. I am about to get up and fry some stuff for breakfast and I . . .' He stops talking and I can hear his clipped breathing down the phone. 'I miss you, Mags. I miss you telling me to fry the bread until it's so crispy there's no chance it will soak up any bean juice. I miss the tea you make to go with the plate of oil that we call a Sunday breakfast. So strong it sticks my tongue to the roof of my mouth. I miss the way you smell.'

I laugh. I can't help myself. Ugly tears are falling down my face.

'The way I smell? On a Sunday morning? You must *really* miss me,' I say through sniffs and splutters.

Neither of us speak for a moment, savouring the moment between happy and the realisation that it's not going to be as easy as that to go back to Sunday morning fry-ups.

'I do . . .' Ed whispers.

'I need to go, Ed,' I say back to him, clearing my throat. 'I have plans today that I can't miss. I'll tell you all about it next time we speak.'

I hear him sigh.

'Thank you, Ed. For calling me to tell me you miss me. Now you go and enjoy your breakfast on your own without the threat of me stealing your sausage.' The breath catches in my throat. 'Are you? You know? On your own.'

Ed scoffs over the phone but I don't pull him up on it. He's called to say he misses me; he's not exactly going to do that if *she's* there, is he?

'Yes, I'm on my own, Maggie. I've been on my own since you left the flat.'

'Oh.' I try not to sound too pleased. 'So . . .'

'Yeah.' I can hear him turning over in bed. 'It felt so wrong, what I did, I couldn't carry on with Annabelle because every time I imagined my future, it was with you; every time I see her all I see is how unlike you she is, and how she can never live up to you because you are my everything. You and me, we just *are*. I don't have to pretend to be someone I'm not with you, because you get me, and I get you.'

'Right,' I say, the ugly tears falling silently again, clogging my throat.

'It's OK, Maggie. I'm not expecting you to immediately forgive me or say these things back to me. But I am not going to stop telling you how I feel. I'm an idiot, I know that now, and I want to make it up to you.'

'Yes, you are,' I squeak through my tears.

He laughs again and I wish he was here, wrapping me in his arms and stroking my hair the way he would when I was crying uncontrollably back at home. Mostly about Gwen or my mum. He'd comfort me and tell me I was worth more than the useless waste of space they made me feel.

But he's not. And I do have plans that I'm not going to cancel just because I'm feeling the emotions triple-fold from a red wine hangover. We say goodbye to each other and I carefully sit up in bed, waiting for the wooziness to kick in. It doesn't. I think I can thank the Ed endorphins for that. I focus on my screen and see it's already half eight. Nick is due at mine at ten and I can't leave him waiting as he's already cancelled his Sunday family stroll to pay me back for the barn visit.

I slip out of the silky sheets – making a mental note to get the make from Perdita – and call a taxi to head home.

★

'So, if you see here . . .' Nick is pointing at his laptop screen and I am trying to look at the tiny lines of data he is showing me without getting so close he can smell last night's hummus on my breath. It's quite hard and I feel light-headed with having to hold my breath. 'There are thousands of people listed in Haverley with the initials LS. I had a go at whittling it down to just men as I assumed your mum was hetero, and there are still *a lot*!'

We're sitting in Mum's kitchen – I'll have moved out and sold the place before I get used to calling it mine again. Nick was full of enthusiasm when he turned up and started working straight away. He'd spread a pile of archived local papers he'd managed to get hold of over the kitchen table and I've been trawling through them to see if there is any mention of my dad. *It's an exciting thing being romantic and fluent in French; well, it's exciting for Haverley, and our home-grown paper loves to do weekend articles on fascinating local people,* Nick had said as he had flicked open the papers for me and pointed at a feature on local asparagus growers. The papers are over the three-year span around the time I think Mum must have got married and I have no idea how he got hold of them so quickly, or indeed at all.

While I trawl the papers, Nick is accessing some old court archives to see if he can find my parents' wedding certificate. If they got married in Haverley then he'll be able to find them pretty quickly. If not, then he said he could pull in a favour from a friend and tapped the side of his nose. A friend with benefits, no doubt. He's probably swapping orgasms for original documents left, right and centre in his job. I don't mind, as long as his sexual exploits end up in him finding my dad. Which is a sentence I never want to hear myself saying again.

His fingers tap away at his keyboard, fast and confident. An image of them working fast and confidently in other ways flashes into my mind and my cheeks burn. He looks at me but doesn't say anything; normally people laugh at my red-hot face when I'm embarrassed, but Nick doesn't seem to care. He probably would if he knew the reason *why* I am embarrassed.

He gets out of his seat and slides open the patio doors, wincing at the screech they've started to make now the nights are getting cooler and the metal is starting to warp. A rush of September morning air flies in and cools my ankles. It's lovely. I feel my face cool off a bit and remember my excitement from yesterday.

'Nick,' I say, leaping out of my seat and coming to stand at the open door beside him, 'you've just reminded me of what I was thinking yesterday.'

'Oh, really?' He raises an eyebrow cheekily at me and I thump him gently on the arm.

'Mind. Gutter!' I say, stepping out into the weeds. 'No, look.'

He looks. He doesn't say anything.

'The garden! We need bunches of wildflowers for your mum's table decorations. They don't get much wilder than this.'

He steps out beside me; neither of us are wearing shoes and I hope that in amongst the weeds aren't vicious thorns ready to spear our feet. Because, as gorgeous as Nick is, I do not want to be picking thorns out of his toes. I hate feet.

'These are perfect, Maggie,' he says, bending down to gently cup the head of a forget-me-not. 'You've got so many colours and sizes here. And they're growing in abundance.'

'Why, thank you,' I say, taking a bow. 'But I think, by definition, that's what weeds do. My inheritance came with a weed-loving gardener who doesn't agree with pesticides.'

'I like her already.'

'It's a he,' I correct him, looking at the back garden with new eyes. 'He's doing it for free, in return for something to do to keep his mind off his late wife. My mum kept him on, apparently, and I'm going to do the same for as long as I have the house. Next time he's here I'll ask him how he feels about helping us help your mum. He'll probably agree if he's given an invite and the bar is free.'

'Thank you, Maggie,' Nick says, turning to me, still caressing the petals of the teeny tiny flowers.

'Anytime,' I say, smiling.

Stop thinking about his hands!

I head back in, treading carefully over the flattened-down path of flowers I've made over the days I've been here. I don't want any more of the pretty flowers to be lost underfoot, though there's plenty to go around. I think the garden must be at least an acre, and most of that looks like the patch just outside the kitchen doors. My creative bones are itching to make something now I've had the idea approved by Nick. But I'm going to wait and get help from the weed master himself. Pops must be busy elsewhere on Sundays as that's the only day he doesn't show up to sweet talk the weeds into growing. Maybe he visits his friends, or his wife's resting place. I sit down and wonder if Ed would visit my grave every week to feel close to me. I think he would. His phone call this morning has shown me he thinks about me when he's going about his everyday life. Because his everyday life was so entwined with mine that to do things without me seems alien. And I can totally understand, because it's how I feel, too.

'Coffee?' Nick asks as he climbs back through the patio doors. I nod, my attention back on the papers.

I'm about halfway through the pile Nick brought with him. He's whistling a tune while he potters about with the kettle, humming the occasional note he can't quite reach with his pursed lips. Ash; 'Girl From Mars'. I recognise it immediately and am thrown back to Sally Morton's party with a jolt.

Chapter Nineteen

Then . . .

'Lighten up, Maggie.' Perdita grabs my hand and gives it a squeeze over the middle seat of her dad's Renault Espace. 'You'll enjoy it when we get there.'

I'm pretty sure I won't, though. Gwen has made my recent days hard enough with her constant berating and reminders that I'm banned from even attending this get together – the last form of fun before I'm thrown into exam mode. I had to sneak out the house to Perdita's on the pretence that we were going to revise, but the look Gwen shot me at the dinner table was enough to make me almost regurgitate my broccoli. I did almost have a pang of guilt at the thought of Gwen having to get up at seven tomorrow to go and interview for a job at an accountancy firm in the city, but I had shoved that down with the broccoli. Besides, Mum was already on the bottle before Gwen and I rustled together some food and the sight of three of her friends staggering up the drive as I left doesn't bode well for Gwen's sleeping arrangements anyway.

I'm wearing a borrowed dress that made Perdita look like Madonna, but it feels itchy and sweaty and I feel like a roll of bin bags. Still, when Perdita had scraped my thick hair back and sprayed it with so much hairspray it now looks neither curly nor auburn, and I added a slick of Rimmel Heather Shimmer lipstick, I decided I looked pretty good.

We've held off covering ourselves with body glitter until we're there as Perdita's dad loves his car probably more than his family. I have a little pot of glitter gel in my bag that we are going to rub down our arms and legs. I might put a bit on my cheekbones, too. Phillip says my cheekbones and pale skin make me look like a member of The Corrs, which made me squeal and hug him in biology last week, much to his horror. I've been practising my Andrea-esque pout ever since. I know Nick Forster is going to be at Sally's party and I really want to make a good impression. I have no idea if he even knows I exist, even though Perdita says he is always staring at me in chemistry. Parties don't seem to be Nick's thing so I've never had the chance to bump into him outside of school. And *nobody*, who is *anybody*, asks someone out in the middle of the day, especially in Mr Bone's chemistry class. Perdita once snuck Phillip a note during a particularly boring class about ions and Mr Bone made her stand at the front of the lab and recite the bloody periodic table.

'Just around the corner, girls,' Mr Greene shouts from the front of the giant people carrier. 'Have you got your bottles of pop? I don't want them left in the car, they might leak.'

'Yes, Dad,' Perdita says, and we both stifle a giggle.

We had tipped out half the contents of the coke and topped it up with my mum's cheapest vodka. She'll never miss it; she gets through enough by herself.

Sally's house is a dream. Whilst my own house might be a sprawling Georgian beast, Sally's house feels happy, like there is a family living there and not just three people who all hate each other inhabiting its walls. Her parents are still together and her dad works for the council, I think; they're away for the weekend, shopping in London, and they don't mind Sally gearing up for the exams with a few friends.

Or the whole of year eleven, and the sixth form by the look of the people spilling out the front door. The house is buzzing. Perdita and I push our way through the hallway to the kitchen at the back of the house, the thrum of Oasis pulsing in my ears. It's jam-packed with people. Hot and sticky, and already the acrid smell of cheap cider is hitting the back of my throat and I keep a tight hold of my vodka. My heart is hammering in my chest, as much as it can whilst being strapped down by a faux leather bodice, and I feel excited and nervous all at once. I grab Perdita's hand and pull her through the throngs of our friends out to the small garden at the back, smiling at people as we go. I feel invincible now. There's a space beside Sally's dad's old BBQ and we fill it, unscrewing the caps off our bottles and swigging. I wince. It's strong.

'Where do you think Phillip is?' I shout at Perdita over 'Champagne Supernova' and loud conversations.

'Probably beside the CD player, deciding what to put on next,' she laughs. 'Where do you think Nick is?'

She winks at me and takes another swig from her bottle. My stomach flips so hard I think I might be sick.

'I'm going to snog him tonight,' I shout back. 'I can feel it.'

A group of girls from our English Language class come and stand with us; we all talk about next year and how hard A levels are going to be. They giggle about universities and how much they're going to miss home. I wish I could say the same, but I can't wait to get away. I swig my vodka and nod occasionally at their premature homesick pangs. Perdita smiles at me. She knows.

The sweet voice of Mark Morriss floods my ears as he sings about being sad and weary. I love Mark Morriss, almost as much as I love Nick Forster. My vodka is empty and I raise the bottle to Perdita and she nods, so I go in search of something to drink that isn't Scrumpy Jack. The kitchen is less busy now; people have moved to the living room and I can hear a loud game of flip cup happening. I hope it's not Brian, the captain of the football team. The last party I was at he drank so much we had to lump him in Sally's mum's wheelbarrow and wheel him three streets over to his own house. I giggle to myself as I remember we tipped him out onto his dad's prize magnolias and ran back to Sally's as fast as we could.

I shout hi to a couple of guys in my maths class and go to check out the bucket where Sally keeps her communal drinks cool. There are a couple of blue WKDs left. I reach for them and my hand bumps into another with the same idea. I look up. The hand belongs to Nick. He smiles at me and I stare at him, too embarrassed to move . . .

Chapter Twenty

The old study is dark this morning, even though I've thrown back the dusty curtains and turned on the bare bulb overhead. I'd been drinking my morning coffee as slowly as possible, waiting for Pops to arrive and get on with his routine of watering and talking to the weeds. I want to ask him for his help with Nick's flowers, but after two cups of coffee and a couple of slices of toast, he still hadn't shown. I've become so used to his presence in the garden, it's strange not to see him on a Monday and I have no way of getting in contact with him to make sure he's OK. So I decided to tackle more paperwork in Mum's old study to see if I can find any details for him, but not before emailing work again as Mr Duncan still hasn't replied to my questions about my return date.

Mum's paperwork mostly consists of newspapers piled high in one corner and still-sealed envelopes scattered over the desk. Rows of shelves with mismatched books and yet more unopened letters. There is a half-filled wastepaper basket topped with a spider's web that looks older than me, given how dusty it is. I have no idea where to even start. The house feels too quiet. I need the distraction of Pops' whistling or the laughter of my friends to pull me out of my thoughts which have sunk to the darkness of the room.

Why did my father not want to know me? Why was Mum so absent throughout my whole life? Why does Gwen hate me so much?

There's a single entity that all of those questions are orbiting around – me. What is it about me that made my family turn against each other? Am I that bad a person that my aura rubs off on people and automatically makes them see I'm a bad person? Is that why Ed decided to find someone else? Though he seems sorry about that now . . . but maybe that's only because I've not been anywhere near him for the last few weeks. He's not been blindsided by my faults and can remember I am a good person really. I wonder if, deep down, I'm not very nice.

I shake my head and try to get out of the fug that is clouding it. Of course I'm a nice person. I have friends who like me and they're kind, generous people. I only came into this dark, stuffy room to try to find a way to get in contact with Pops because I am worried about him. Would a selfish person do that? I need to stop questioning myself. And I need to get out of this room.

I shut the door behind me and walk down the hallway, back through to the kitchen. My heart lifts as I see Pops and his watering can. The noise the door makes as I slide it open hurts my fillings, but the sight of the garden and the wash of fresh air and sunshine more than makes up for it.

'Pops!' I shout over the weeds. 'I was getting worried I hadn't seen you.'

'Morning, Maggie love.' He waves with his free hand. 'Put the kettle on, would you? I'm gasping. Thought you'd forgotten about me today.'

I laugh and go and make him a cuppa and he stops his work to take it from me.

'I was feeling a bit tired this morning,' he says, sipping his tea. 'Took me a while to get going. But I'm raring now.'

He makes a noise like a motorbike revving, only it sounds like his chest is making most of the noise.

'Are you feeling OK enough to be here?'

His laugh makes the rattle sound worse. I raise an eyebrow and take the watering can from his hands.

'Wait here,' I command. And I return a few moments later with a couple of chairs, putting them carefully in the gaps I made a few days ago with Perdita and Phillip. 'Sit.'

'You're worse than the wife,' he says, but he sits down.

I wonder if he's missing her more and that's why he's not at his best. Or if he's actually poorly.

'Pops,' I ask, 'do you think you'd be able to help Nick and me with something from the garden?'

Pops raises an eyebrow at me.

'Nick? Nick Forster would that be, by any chance?' His lopsided grin tells me all I need to know about what he thinks we're up to. I ignore the lewd look.

'It's his mum's sixtieth birthday and he's organising the party. He asked for my help to make it look good, and I thought maybe we could use some of the flowers in the garden as decorations.'

I explain a bit more about the barn and the need to keep the costs down, leaving out why. It's not my place to tell other peoples' family stories. God knows I have enough of my own. As I'm talking, I'm wondering if Pops might not want us to use his carefully tended weeds. Without the garden, what would he have left? I add quickly that there would be lots left for him to care for, but he seems undeterred.

'Ivy Forster is turning sixty? Well I never. Of course, I'd be happy to help. It will be lovely to see the flowers used for such a great cause.'

With a renewed vigour he jumps out of his chair and grabs the scissors in his belt. He's off into the wild before I can say comfrey.

My phone vibrates in my pocket.

Quick question? What's worse? Nose for toes or toes for nose.

It's Ed. I laugh. We used to play this game when we were bored. Airports or train stations were a classic. But sometimes late at night as we were trying to fall asleep, wrapped in each other's arms, Ed would fire off a silly game of *would you rather* and we'd end up laughing about it for hours, cursing ourselves the next morning because we were tired after difficult decision-making over whether we wanted to only eat one meal for the rest of our lives or lots of meals but everything tastes the same.

Given the way your feet smell, if I were you, I'd opt for toes for nose.

Good point. Imagine having to smell my feet all day every day.

I don't have to imagine, I can remember.

It feels good to be having this conversation. It's normal, and jokey, and light. As though it's bypassing the seriousness and reminding me of why Ed and I worked so well in the first place. Before me and my inner rot had chased him into the arms, or legs, of another woman.

Pops returns with a posy in his hand and a smile on his face.

'How about something like this?' he asks, setting the posy in my hand.

It's awash with colour, blues and whites and yellows. It looks straight from the pages of *Anne of Green Gables*; all it needs is a tie of chequered ribbon and a jam jar, and it will be perfect for the party. A big fluffy bumblebee comes to check it out and I watch as it flies in and out of the little petals, marvelling at how its tiny wings can keep its huge body in the air.

'This is perfect, Pops,' I say when the bee has flown off. 'You've done this before.'

'Once or twice,' he shrugs, smiling.

'Would it be OK for me to recreate this a few times over for the party? Do you mind if I use the flowers?'

He laughs and sits back down in the chair I'd got for him, taking great gulps of what must be cold coffee.

'They're your flowers, love.'

'They're not really, though, are they?' I say. 'You're the one who looks after them. I would have mown them all down and had a table and chairs out here if you'd left it to me.'

Pops pretends to cover the flowers with his hands.

'Don't listen to her, my pretties,' he says. 'She's joking.' He turns to me. 'I'm happy to help you make the flower decorations if you'd like me to? Does the party have a free bar?'

His question has me laughing all the way back into the house as I rinse our mugs. I want to tell Nick that I had guessed Pops' bartering correctly but my fingers hover over the screen of my phone, momentarily awash with the guilt of messaging another very attractive man while Ed is obviously trying so hard to make things OK between us. But I'm not messaging Nick because I want to get in his trousers; plus, I want to see how he's getting on with translating the love between my parents. I dash out a quick message to Nick to let him know we are all go with the flowers and drop Ed a kiss while I'm at it. Guilt overridden.

The rest of the day I spend pottering around, washing down the kitchen windows, hoovering the downstairs, the living room, the study, the old dining room that was never used, and the kitchen. I draw the line at the toilet because the old lino looks as though it would be sucked up into the vacuum bag if I went anywhere near it. I find a new duster and half a can of Mr Sheen under the kitchen sink, so I set about dusting as many of the surfaces as I can get to. Then I tuck myself onto the sofa in the living room with a cup of tea and Mum's old copy of *The Woman in White*, creeping myself out when the pipes creak and groan or the mice start chewing away at the floorboards underneath me. I had thrown open the sash windows in the room and my reading has the background music of the birds singing to each other in the trees lining the driveway.

This is a beautiful family home. Despite the multitude of memories that are less than positive, I can draw on the times with Perdita and Phillip to remember the house as happy for me, too. My childhood was shaped by loss rather than love, but it was one that I do have fond memories of.

At a particularly creepy bit in my book, I pull my phone out and start scrolling Google for ways to find lost family members. It feels glib, like I could have been doing this ages ago if I really wanted to. But the letters and the initials have injected back a little of the hope that Mum had sucked out of me with a straw and some relish. An ancestry site entices me in with a free week's worth of searches and I throw my own details on the page before I change my mind. As I hit send my phone vibrates with a message.

Sorry I've taken so long to reply. I had to pull in a favour with a friend. Your parents can't have been married in Norfolk, there are no marriages around the time with those initials, and I checked an entire decade. I'm widening the search area. Any more luck with the newspapers?

I feel all sorts of confusion at Nick's message. The thought that he is pulling in favours for one – not that I should mind. I don't think I do mind. I really shouldn't mind, because he's doing it for me and I'm jumping to conclusions about the way he's pulling in these favours anyway, with his muscly arms and his cheeky grin and his wayward curls. Ed's smiling face pops into my head and tries to shut down those thoughts and focus instead on the guilt that Nick is working hard to find my dad and I'm sitting here with Wilkie Collins and Google. I head back to the kitchen and the pile of newspapers I haven't yet looked through. Pops' posy looks gorgeous in the shot glass I'd filled with water and put on the table. I snap a photo and send it to Nick.

No luck with the papers yet but Pops did this.

I wait to hear back, but Nick must be very busy calling in this favour as my phone stays quiet until later that evening.

Les roses sont rouges
Les violettes sont bleues
Mon coeur me fera mal
Être loin de toi

Roses are red
Violets are blue
My heart will ache
Being away from you

Chapter Twenty-One

'I thought the *flowers* were going to be my job?' I say to Nick as he drives us into the city.

'*One* of your jobs, Maggie,' he says, concentrating on the road, trying to find a good time to overtake the combine harvester that has been in front of us for the last few miles. He's tapping his fingers on the wheel and the speed of the noise is making me hyper aware of the slowness of the car.

He'd picked me up from the house. But before I'd even thrown some stuff in my bag to go, he'd whipped out a spray can of WD-40 and sorted the kitchen doors for me. There is something guarded about him this morning, though. An impenetrable force field I've not felt with him before, and it's followed us to the car.

'Is everything OK?' I ask.

He's in jeans and a shirt, the sleeves rolled up to his elbows giving me a great view of the muscles in his tanned forearms as he taps his fingers and holds on to the wheel.

'What?' He looks at me, as though only just registering that he's not alone in the car. 'Sorry. Yes. No. I don't know. While I was out yesterday, with the friend who's helping me search the marriage records, Dad took a turn for the worse. Mum couldn't find him, then we both searched and had no luck. Turns out he'd walked through Haverley to the pub he used to go to with his best mate. He was in his socks and his pyjamas; luckily the weather was good, but what if he'd wandered into the road, or it had been thick snow. What then?'

'Oh Nick, that must have been really scary for you all. Was he OK?'

'Yeah, the barman called Mum to let her know as soon as Dad walked in the door. He gave him a half of pale ale, just like he used to drink, so Dad was happy. We're lucky we have a good community here, but I'm worried about him and Mum. It's scary to think of the what ifs and the maybes. And Mum is looking permanently exhausted. What if Dad's wanderings get worse and he ends up in the pub every day? Although, he did have a whale of a time so he'd probably be OK with that. He was playing darts by the time Mum and I turned up to collect him. He's still a good shot, luckily.'

Nick laughs. 'Sorry, I don't mean to bring the mood down. I'll try to lighten up a bit.'

'Nick, you don't need to lighten up for me. I just wanted to check you were OK because you seemed a bit tense. But now I know why, you don't need to suddenly be OK. It's OK to not be OK, or whatever that corny but very true saying is.'

Nick clears his throat and I want to say something else, something less glib. But I also don't want to witter on like an idiot and make things more tense. So I keep quiet as Nick drives us into a multi-storey car park and parks neatly in a bay between two large SUVs. The action makes my skin ripple in goosebumps. I've always had a thing for a good driver – I think it's the confidence that sets my pulse racing. Perdita just thinks it's because I'm weird.

Nick is confident in everything he does, I know that now. I couldn't see that at school because he was confi-dent doing things that weren't cool. He's grown into the sensitive man sitting next to me feeling low because his dad's mind is deteriorating, from the sensitive boy he was growing up. Never once did he make fun of me for my lack of common sense, or the heat that would radiate from my face whenever he came near me. He was simply Nick.

He looks at me looking at him and my cheeks heat. Once again, I'm thankful for my thoughts being contained inside my head and not on show for all and sundry.

'Shall we?' he asks.

'Let's,' I nod.

We wander through the cobbled streets of the city, staying in the older part where the shops are independent and the buildings are wonky. I love it here, it feels more personable than London. But that's why I left, wasn't it? To get away from personable and blend into a city of strangers.

The streets are emptier now than they have been in the last few weeks. Kids have returned to school and their parents are sleeping for weeks to make up for the summer holidays or, more likely, deep-cleaning the soft furnishings and steam-cleaning the bathroom.

'Shouldn't you be at work?' I ask Nick as we stop to look in the window of a fudge shop.

'I've taken a couple of weeks off to sort Mum's party. And help with Dad. And you now, too,' he says, smiling at me in the reflection in the window.

I can't help but smile back at his face, dotted with rum and raisin and mint choc chip squares of sugary fudge. Sweet. We stay for a moment, looking into each other's reflected smiles. I feel the muscles in my chest restrict as my breath catches in my throat. A knot of excitement is threatening to burst out of me from where it has been buried deep, dormant since high school. Until a bald head appears at the window and asks if we need any help. I squeal and jump away from the glass, laughing so hard at the scare. Nick is less chaotic in his reply to the shop owner and we head off before he comes out and sweeps us away with a broom like street urchins in a Dickensian novel. Nick certainly looks the part.

He offers me his arm and I take it as he leads me down an alleyway flanked by flint walls and perfect iron lamp posts.

'I signed myself up to an ancestry website,' I say, smelling the sweet smell of hog roast as it crackles over one of the walls. 'Just to help in the search for my dad. I haven't had a chance to look yet, but I'll get on it later tonight.'

'Good idea; I'll do some more translating later, too, and some more searching,' Nick says, squeezing my arm with his. 'Though if you find out you're related to King Henry VIII, please don't chop off my head for all my sins.'

I snort. I want him to list his sins so I can hear it from the horse's mouth, so to speak, but he leads me into a perfect Norfolk flint church masquerading as an antique shop.

'OK, dear Maggie, it's time to go wild.'

I take a look about the church, obese royalty long forgotten. A couple of pensioners with plastic hair covers are perusing the oddities at one of the stalls, but other than that it's deserted.

'Wild,' I say, the corner of my mouth lifting in glee.

'Hey.' He nudges me gently with his elbow. 'Don't knock my favourite pastime. I need you to help me find some antique-y looking jars for the flowers. And maybe a decoration or two, I don't know.'

'Haven't you heard of Amazon?' I laugh.

'Shut up, Margaret! Use your wily female senses to pick out a few things to make the barn look sixtieth birthday ready for a person who loves knitting and yoga – and the occasional whodunnit murder-mystery party where she can dress up like Poirot and make us drink Cosmopolitans out of original fifties cocktail glasses.'

'She sounds like my kind of person,' I say, taking a look at the stalls from a distance, wondering where to start.

'I think she'd love you, too,' Nick says, stuttering slightly, and he whips his head towards the door we've just come in and mutters something about the weather.

I leave him to it and start wandering through the stalls, determined to get some beautiful things for Mrs Forster's party. There are trinkets galore, vintage clothes – things that would probably sell on *Bargain Hunt* for a lot more than they're selling for here if they're spotted by the right pair of eyes. Not mine, by the way. I can't spot a Dickenson's Real Deal, but I can spot a stall full of crockery and, dotted in between the cups and saucers, are small jam jars that look the right size to hold one of Pops' posies.

I hunt around for Nick and spot him talking to an eager-looking stallholder on the younger side of the spectrum.

'Nick?' I say, not really wanting to disturb him but he turns to me and says his goodbyes to the stallholder. She turns a lovely shade of pink and I roll my eyes at his innocent shrug. 'Is this like that moment in *Pretty Woman* where Julia Roberts is allowed to shop with Richard's credit card? Only I've found some beautiful jam jars that I think would work really well but I'm not sure how much I have to spend.'

Nick gives me a little smirk.

'I'd pretend I haven't seen the film, but that would be a massive lie and I don't do lies. So as long as we're not going to get arrested for solicitation then, like I said, go wild.'

'Solicitation? This escalated quickly. What about if we have sex and you *don't* pay me, what then?' I wink back at him, carried along by his flirtatious verve.

I can feel the air between us fizz with energy.

'Then that's fair game, I guess,' he replies, holding my eyes and moving so close to me I can feel the warmth of his breath. 'Though let's not do that here, we don't want to give the old dears a coronary.'

He makes this easy. My insides feel all warm and fuzzy. I turn to go back and buy the jam jars but Nick's hand reaches out and grabs my wrist. His touch on my bare skin is like fire and the playful flirting has switched up a gear. I can feel my pulse thrumming in my throat, blocking my swallow, and restricting my air.

'Maggie,' he says, his voice all throaty, and I wait for him to tell me how he's forgiven me for breaking his heart all those years ago at high school, and then I'll have to break it all over again because Ed. Ed! 'When I say *go wild*, try to keep it under forty quid, then we'll have enough left for coffee.'

He puts a bunch of folded notes into my hand and lets go of me, completely unaware of how he is making me feel. I breathe, suddenly remembering how.

Chapter Twenty-Two

'Let's go for a coffee,' Nick says, both of us laden with bags that clink with precariously balanced jam jars.

'Good idea,' I say in clipped words, handing him back the change.

I'm trying to be more formal because I have to think of Ed. Flirting isn't ruled out, but the way it's making me feel definitely crosses a line. Nick's smile falters slightly at the tone of my voice, but he leads me out of the church and over the green to a coffee shop with a scattering of chairs and tables outside.

'Have a seat – what would you like?' he asks, carefully planting his own bags by the leg of one of the tables.

'Flat white, please,' I say, putting mine next to his and taking a seat so I can look out over the city.

He disappears into the coffee shop and I take a moment to reset my thinking, bring myself down from the high I've been feeling. Nick has made me settle back in Norfolk like it's home. He's a comfy sweater that I reach for at the end of a hard day, a kind word that lifts my spirits. He's always so relaxed, so open. Everything about the way he is, his confidence, the way he looks at people, holds their eyes. He treats me as an equal, a friend, as though I'd never left the county, yet it's been over a decade since we last spoke. People pass by, not noticing me as I sit pondering awkwardly how Nick and I left things back then.

'Here we go,' Nick says, putting a tray of drinks on the table. My coffee slops over the side of my mug and makes a pool of hot black liquid around the bottom. 'I got you hot and cold milk because I wasn't sure which one you'd prefer.'

He puts my mug in front of me with some sugar and a couple of metal jugs, one with frothy milk that smells like bedtime. I pour the hot milk over my coffee and pick it up, cradling it in my hands. My permanently freezing fingertips warm up. Nick picks up his own. Black coffee. He doesn't add any milk or sugar.

'Right, Maggie,' Nick says, 'your eye for a bargain and keen detail leads me to want to ask you for help buying Mum's present.'

He grins at me so the dimples in his cheeks dent like black holes drawing me in with their anti-gravitational pull.

'Have you not bought your mum a present yet? Her party's in four days!'

'I've had a few ideas,' he whines. 'And I have been a bit distracted of late. But, yes, you're right to talk to me like a child.'

He laughs and I bat him on the shoulder, my awkwardness dissipating with his smiles.

'We can have these and then maybe head to some shops to get a few ideas?' I say, liking the idea of ironing out my feelings for Nick while I'm still with him.

Then another image of Ed flashes into my mind and I feel guilt slosh around my stomach with the coffee.

'So, Ed and I are patching things up,' I blurt. I don't know why I'm telling Nick this. Only it feels important that he knows.

'Right. I did wonder when I heard you talking to him the other day. That's good.' He sips at his coffee, his eyes finding mine over the rim of his cup.

'It is good,' I say, dropping my eyes to my own empty cup. 'It is.'

'Right,' he says, flexing his muscles like the Incredible Hulk. 'Let's go and buy my mum a gift.'

Chapter Twenty-Three

'You stay here,' Nick whispers. 'I want to go and check it's safe.'

It's dusk by the time we get back to the house and, as we had turned onto the driveway, my body had tensed as I saw lights on in the hallway and the study. I was adamant I hadn't left them on, what with Gwen's constant reminders that the electricity and gas bills will be mine alone while I'm staying at the house, I'd been more energy conscious than David Attenborough. Nick had made glib comments about unqualified burglars, but to be fair, he was offering to protect me. The car made such a racket crunching over the gravel of the drive, and the headlights are still shining so brightly into the study window, that I think any burglar worth his salt would have hot-footed it over the weeds at the back and be halfway to Ipswich by now. But Nick's chivalrous offer is too good to refuse.

'I'll let you lead, but I'm not staying in the car,' I whisper conspiratorially back, glancing around the car for baddies. 'Have you never watched a horror movie? Don't split up. Ever. And especially don't leave the girl alone. I might do something stupid, like run into the woods barefoot, with only a nightie on.'

A little snort emits from between Nick's lips.

'That's a sight worth leaving you alone in the car for.'

'Oi,' I protest, just a little too lightly. 'You never want to see me running in a nightie. Trust me. There is not enough material in a nightie. Actually, scrap that. You never want to see me running. Period.'

We both laugh. Then I remember I am supposed to be checking out who is lurking around Mum's house and I sober up pretty quickly.

I open the car door and shut it with the stealth of a rhino, wincing at Nick's expression and mouthing *sorry*. With the engine off and the lights gone, it does feel a little more sinister out here now. The sun is dipping behind the back of the house, so the woods at the front of the house look tall and dense. The woods I will definitely not be running through, even fully clothed. But the fading light is not quite enough to illuminate the front door properly. It may only be September, but in the middle of the countryside we're not high tech enough for streetlights, so when there's no sun, there's no light. It's a great way to learn about science, living in the countryside.

Nick reaches the front door and turns back to me.

'I can't go in, I don't have a key,' he whispers.

The stifled giggles that ensue are the kind that I used to have when I was younger, when Perdita and I would head home from the pub trying not to make too much noise as we toasted bread and slathered it with butter. My sides ache and the tears streaming down my cheeks are hot. Nick's face is puce and he's doubled over like he needs to wee. My hands shake as I rummage around in the near darkness for my key. Nick pig snorts with the effort of trying to keep as quiet as possible and our laughter doubles in size. By the time I've got the door open I'm ready to lie down with the effort. Nick steps in front again and I follow, still bent double and hanging off the waist of his jeans to keep myself upright. His body shakes with a silent laughter I can feel through his belt.

'Is there anybody there?' Nick shouts feebly, and that's enough to push me over the edge.

'Seriously, Nick! Again, have you never seen a horror movie?' I cry through my tears. 'This is the point where the maniacal axe murderer jumps out and hacks you down and sends me fleeing half-naked into the woods.'

'What, no nightie anymore? Best start stripping now then,' he splutters, just as the door to the study bursts open and I think I might actually wee myself.

We jump backwards and Nick lands on my toe. With a yelp I push him off me and right into whoever has just walked out into the hallway with us.

'What on earth is going on here?' demands a voice I recognise.

'Ed?' I say, bolting upright and definitely not laughing now.

The three of us stand there for what feels like a lifetime. Nick and I move further apart, repelled as though we've just been caught doing something we shouldn't and not the other way around.

'What's going on here?' Ed asks again, looking between me and Nick like we're playing tennis and he's a spectator at Wimbledon with his strawberries and cream.

'I thought the house was being burgled, so Nick offered to help,' I say, my face heating with the force I am putting into not looking guilty. 'How did you get in?'

'I used the key under the duck, like always!' Ed says. 'And what do you mean, burgled?'

'There were lights on – but what have you got there?'

Now Ed has the grace to look guilty as he eyeballs the stack of paperwork in his hands.

'I was looking for some candles and I was moving these out of a drawer to get a better look. I thought the house was empty. I mean, I came to see you but when I arrived the house *seemed* empty. I came to see you. To apologise properly.'

'I think I'm going to leave you two to it,' Nick says, reminding me he is still in the hallway. 'Thanks for your help today, Maggie.'

He shuts the door quietly behind him and the hallway descends into silence. I can hear the ticking of the clock in the living room and the steady drip of a leak that must have sprung up somewhere in the house. Ed moves closer to me, the smell of him familiar, his aftershave and soap.

'It's good to see you,' Ed says, his eyes still on the closed door over my shoulder.

I can tell he's itching to ask me about Nick but maybe he feels it's not his place to start questioning me on who I'm spending time with. I feel an affinity towards Ed for managing to keep his mouth shut.

'It's good to see you, too,' I say, and with relief I realise I mean it.

It *is* good to see him. I stop standing on ceremony and wrap my arms around his familiar shape, drawing him closer to me. He kisses the top of my head and hugs me harder.

'I'm so sorry, Maggie,' he whispers.

I don't reply, because I don't want to think about that right now. This hug is too full of future promises to think about past mistakes. I tilt my head up and Ed brings his lips towards mine. For a split second the image of him kissing Annabelle flits over my eyes, but I shush it away with the endorphins still rushing around my body. Then Ed kisses me and all thoughts of everything and anything are expelled from my head with the rush of longing I feel.

His hands grab my face as he kisses me harder, his tongue seeking out mine. I can't draw him close enough to me, though my arms are pulling him against my body. My body. It's obvious that my body has forgotten about whatever mistakes have happened. I want Ed. And he wants me.

There's no time to make it upstairs. The urgency is too great. We grab at each other's clothes, trying to get rid of them, to be next to each other without all the baggage. My jeans are too tight to get below my knees, so we leave them there, hanging off my legs like a snake's half-shed skin. We stumble together as one, through the door to the living room and make it to the sofa. Ed's hands are in my hair now, his fingers wrapped in it, holding me tightly. My fingers are shaking too much to undo his belt so he stops, for a second that feels like a whole lifetime, to undo the buckle himself. My cheeks feel like they're burning and the fire roaring a lot further down my body is heating the rest of me like a furnace.

Then Ed is on top of me, the old sofa groaning under the weight of us, Ed groaning at the weight of what is happening. I clear my mind and enjoy the connection until we're a sweaty mass of body, breathing in sync, exhausted and happy. We collapse on the sofa together, wrapped in each other's arms like old times, and drift into a safe sleep . . .

I'm woken by my phone buzzing, what must be a few hours later, as the room is pitch black and the birds have stopped their bedtime songs. I fumble over my jeans, dragging them off over my ankles and pulling my knickers back up. I feel around on the floor for my vest and pull it over my head. Ed is still fast asleep. Even the way he is snoring is familiar in a comforting way. The gentle guttering, in with a stutter, out with a whistle. It makes me feel like I'm at home. *My* home. The flat I have shared with Ed, not this dilapidated old house. My shin hits against a coffee table, the swear I want to shout contained carefully inside until I've felt my way out to the hallway.

'Shit, ow,' I say, rubbing the sore bit.

I don't want to wake Ed up, not if I don't need to. I left my bag by the front door, my phone, inside it, vibrates angrily again.

Who is messaging me at this time of night?

I find it, illuminating the sweet wrappers and old pens at the bottom of my bag. It's only eleven, so whoever it is I'll let them off.

Sorry if today got awkward between you and Ed. Thanks for your help. Muchos appreciated. If you want to give me Pops' details, I can organise the flowers directly with him, if that's easier.

Nick! I send him back a reply, walking through to the kitchen to put the kettle on as I do.

No way, you're not taking over flower duty. Today was fun.
x

I read it over, delete the kiss and send it.

Chapter Twenty-Four

'And this one here is the one I found first.'

Ed is lying in bed, naked, covered up by the summer duvet curled at his waist. The morning sun is streaming in through the window. I've got my dad's notes out and have been reading them out to him in my Norfolk version of French, the romance making me feel alive. That and the numerous times Ed and I have had sex since we moved upstairs. I'm buzzing with happy pheromones that even Gwen wouldn't be able to shake off.

'*J'taime*,' Ed reads and turns to me, his eyebrow raised. 'Why on earth would anybody sane send your mum *one* love letter, let alone *eight*?'

He snorts and reads it again, this time in his head. I feel a pang of annoyance at his attack of my mum, especially as she's not here to defend herself anymore. But he is right, it was my first thought, too, after the excitement of the idea of a dad. My friends had said something similar, so had Nick, and he hadn't really known my mum, he just knew her reputation. So I try not to let the bubble of irritation pop at Ed.

'But aren't they romantic?' I ask, leaning on his shoulder and giving him a peck on the cheek. 'Nick's helping me translate them so we can look for my dad. He's the guy who was here yesterday. I'm helping him with his mum's party in return.'

'How do you know him?' Ed asks, his eyes darkening almost imperceptibly.

Irritating though it is, I kind of like the fact he's getting jealous.

'We went to school together. Haven't seen him for almost twenty years.' I omit my schoolgirl crush.

Ed's cheeks pink. 'Has anything happened between you? He is, you know, an attractive guy. I wouldn't blame you.'

I flip over on to my front and trace my finger down Ed's chest, the soft, blond hair parting as I go. Ed puts down the letters on his bedside table and covers my hand in his.

'Ed,' I say quietly, 'I never stopped loving you. I couldn't imagine being with someone else. And give me credit, he may be attractive but I've only been here a few weeks!'

Ed brings my hand up to his lips and kisses it.

'I am never going to make that mistake again. I'm so sorry, Maggie.'

'What happened with Annabelle?' I need to ask otherwise my imagination will run away with me.

'She wasn't you,' Ed says. 'I think I got cold feet. I was worried that my life was running away without me. House, marriage, kids. Soon I'd be old and I felt that I wanted to make some decisions that I had taken myself.'

He sighs and shifts up in bed. I roll back over and pull the duvet up to my chin. I know what he means, I've felt the same about my own life. As though someone else is making the decisions. But, to me, that feels good. My parental decision-makers were non-existent growing up, so it is freeing to finally be able to hand the reins over to someone else. Even if that *someone* is just a fallacy of the normal path of a life well-trodden. Normal is safe to me, and that's fine.

'I'm sorry, this is all coming out wrong,' Ed says, running his hands through his hair. 'I'm not saying that the decisions I made with and about you were not what I wanted, I *do* want to make even more decisions with you. Bigger decisions. But I felt like my life was mapped out in front of me whether I liked it or not, and that scared me. But I know now I had no reason to be scared, because everything I needed was right in front of me.'

'A bit like Justin Timberlake when he wrote that song about Jessica Biel?'

I roll back over and start to sing the part about being right here all along. My singing voice at the best of times is average, and first thing in the morning is not the best of times. Ed laughs.

'See,' he says, pulling the covers down from my neck and kissing my collarbone until my skin starts going all goosebumpy, 'this is why I love you. You can make me laugh and smile – and even your singing voice does this to me.'

He lifts the covers up and lets me see just how much he likes my singing voice.

'I can sing some more if you'd like me to?' I simper, hilariously.

Ed kisses me. 'Nope,' he says, dotting his words between kisses. 'There's no need for that.'

And he rolls on top of me as I start singing 'Cry Me a River'.

'Morning, Pops!' I shout through the kitchen window as I fill the kettle.

'It's nearly midday,' he shouts back, looking pointedly at the place on his tanned arm where a watch might live.

I throw open the window behind the sink.

'Nick says he loves the flowers and you've got a deal. Just don't hog the whisky. Are you free on Friday to make up some bunches with me, and I'll drop them at the venue on Saturday morning?'

'Yep,' Pops says, leaning on the handle of the rake, small droplets of sweat forming on his wrinkly brow. It's the first time I've seen him with an actual gardening tool that isn't a watering can.

'I got some jars yesterday to put them in. I think you'll approve.'

'Right.'

'Man of many words this morning, Pops.'

His chest rises and falls as he mops his brow with an old embroidered hanky from his top pocket.

'Good family, the Forsters,' he says eventually. 'They always look out for others. Who's this?'

I feel arms around my waist and Ed kisses my neck, drawing me in for a standing spoon.

'Ed,' I say to Pops, whose face has turned sour. I hope he's feeling OK; he looks like he's going to keel over. 'Pops, meet my boyfriend Ed; Ed, this is Pops, the wonderful gardener I've been telling you about.'

'You never mentioned him,' Ed whispers in my ear and I nudge him in the ribs with an elbow. 'Hi, Pops.'

'Yes, we met at Elizabeth's funeral,' Pops says in reply and Ed pretends he remembers.

Pops' normally outdoorsy tanned face has turned the colour of old grey laundry.

'Are you OK?' I bite my tongue as it comes out, remembering how he disliked my questioning last time. 'Sorry, I'll get on with your coffee.'

I pull the window shut. Ed has taken himself off to the table with the newspaper. He must have brought it with him because it's a *Metro* and not the local *Eastern Daily Press* that my mum used to get. I put a mug down in front of him and he grunts a thanks, just like old times. But he reaches for my hand as I turn, stopping me, pulling me back down for a kiss.

'I mean,' he says, kissing my nose, 'thank you for my coffee, love. I'm trying. But you'll have to ignore me when I slip back into my old ways. No more taking you for granted.'

I practically skip out the door with Pops' drink, though I don't want to spill it all over my hand and end up in A & E.

'Yes,' Pops says as I hand him his drink. 'They're a good family, the Forsters.'

It's a funny thing to say to me, but Pops looks a little away with the garden gnomes today and I think he might have been on the juice already this morning, so I don't pay much heed to his words. Though, with the help that Nick is giving me in finding my dad and the work he does for vulnerable people, I can tell for myself that he has a good heart.

'Mags,' Ed is shouting me from the table, 'your phone is ringing.'

Better bloody not be Gwen again, I think as I take it from Ed's hands.

There is only so much chastising I can be doing with in a twenty-four-hour period, and I reached that a good few hours ago.

'Maggie?' It's Nick. He sounds out of breath and I wonder briefly where he went after he left Ed and me alone last night and if he's had to hotfoot it home this morning.

'Hi, Nick, everything OK?'

Ed eyes me suspiciously and I turn to the door and watch Pops work as I talk, conscious of Ed listening behind me.

'Yes! Maggie,' Nick says, 'I think I may have found something.'

'About my dad?' I squeak.

'Yes. It's a wedding certificate. Not Norfolk, but my friend came through. It's the seventies, so the right-ish dates and the female is Elizabeth Burnett. The guy is somebody called Leonard Simpson. Look, it's probably not something to go over on the phone, so let's get Mum's party out of the way and we can start searching for this Leonard. We might have him, Mags. We might have found your dad.'

I look back round at Ed who's watching me. My face feels hot with the excitement that in the next few weeks I might know who my father is. Nick has worked his magic and has found a family member who might actually like to spend time with me, once he gets to know me.

'Nick, you're amazing!' I shout, and Ed gets out of his seat and comes over to hug me. 'Thank you so much. I owe you more than flowers from my garden for this.'

Ed squeezes me tight.

'No, don't be silly,' Nick says, and I swap the phone to my other ear so it's further away from Ed's face. 'Reuniting you with your dad will be more than enough thanks for me. See you soon, Maggie. I've got to go, Dad's trying to find the lawnmower again.'

I ring off as Nick starts talking to his dad in the background, not wanting to intrude. But I couldn't help but overhear him as he spoke softly to his dad, telling him that the hoover doesn't work outside.

'That sounded exciting,' Ed says into my ear, still holding me tightly in a bear hug from behind.

Wriggling free I turn to face him. Nerves are making my fingers twitch and my feelings jangle.

'Nick thinks he might have found Mum and Dad's wedding certificate. We might be able to find my dad now,' I say, tears pricking at my eyes.

'Oh, Mags, that's amazing news,' Ed says, wrapping me up in his arms again.

I want to enjoy the hug, but my body is itching to move. It's as though my limbs want to shake in every direction at the gravity of the news Nick has just given me. Excitement and nerves are flowing through me and that is not good for being squashed in a hug, no matter how delicious the hug is. I wriggle free again and kiss Ed on the lips. Now I'm free, though, I have no idea what to do with my body because shaking it out like I'm just about to start a yoga class seems a bit too normal for the news.

This is it. This could be the start of a new relationship with my dad.

Quand mes yeux t'ont aperçu pour la première fois, j'ai pensé que tu étais un rêve. Maintenant je sais que tu ne l'es pas, tu es tellement plus que je ne pourrais l'imaginer moi-même.

When my eyes first caught sight of you, I thought you were a dream. Now I know you're not, you're so much more than I could imagine on my own.

Chapter Twenty-Five

My mum's dress reaches all the way past my feet. My newly painted coral nails poke out from underneath, their brightness a stark contrast to the midnight-blue silk. I had to pin the little ruffle sleeves at their base, as Mum was broader than I am, but other than that, it fits like a glove. With my hair pinned back and rather more makeup than I have worn in at least three months, I am party ready. I snap a quick picture and send it to the besties group chat so I have it as proof I can scrub up well.

I feel good. Ed and I have been talking. He has been attentive the last few days, as though scared to let me out of his sight. I'm still taking it one step at a time, but I feel like there has been a huge shift in my thinking. Helped along by the amazing news Nick gave me, I've been adding my family's data into the ancestry website and seeing where it takes me, which isn't far, as I've only got three people, plus Mum's parents who died really young. I'm itching to get started looking for my dad with Nick, but first I have a party to get to.

'Mags!' Ed shouts up the stairs. 'Pops is here.'

We're sharing a taxi to the party because we all want to make good use of the free bar, and because none of us has a car. I hitch up the dress, thankful that Mum had such a party-ready wardrobe, and head down to where Ed has been panic-drinking while I've been getting ready. I've not seen him this nervous about a party in forever.

'Wow, Miss Burnett, you look like a sight for sore eyes,' Pops calls from the bottom of the staircase as I descend. He wipes his eyes with the back of his hand.

I notice he's not dressed for a party, but I don't want to say anything in case this *is* his party wear. He still has his gardening tool belt around his middle; in fact, his whole get-up is what he was wearing yesterday when we picked the flowers and arranged them in the jars, gardener-chic. He'd brought some twine with him and wrapped a few strands around the neck of the jars which made them look as if they'd been arranged by an editor of *House and Country* magazine and not a townie and an octogenarian weed-lover.

'Thank you, Pops,' I say, taking his hands in mine and squeezing them excitedly.

Up close he looks pale and his hands feel cold and clammy. I look at him with concern.

'I'm not going to make the party, love,' he says, holding my arms up so he can see my dress properly. 'I think I must be fighting a cold and I don't want to spread my germs to the lovely Forsters. Please can you send them my love?'

'Oh, Pops,' I say, saddened by his news, 'of course I can. We'll miss you loads and loads. I'll be sure to raid the bar on your behalf.'

His eyes crinkle in a smile and I can hear Ed approach from the kitchen.

'Bloody hell, Maggie, you look ravishing.' Ed has a glass of what could be gin and tonic in each hand. 'Let's skip the party, hey?'

I blush and look at the floor, embarrassed by his openness in front of Pops who looks cheekily at both of us.

'It would be a shame not to share that beauty with others, though, wouldn't it, Ed?' he says, winking at me as he rubs my arm. 'I think that's the taxi I can hear. You kids have fun.'

I walk ahead as Ed pays for the taxi. Little tea lights lead the way up towards the barn which is itself illuminated by what could be a million fairy lights. The roof sparkles like it's Christmas, but it's warm and no white-bearded man will be climbing down *this* chimney. I can see throngs of people through the large window, milling about, casually talking to each other, glasses in their hands, heads thrown back in laughter. I'm itching to get inside, but my nerves are getting the better of me so I wait for Ed to catch up and grab his arm.

'You're shivering, Mags,' he says, throwing his arm around my shoulder. 'Cold?'

'No,' I say as a shiver runs all the way to my toes. 'Excited. Nervous.'

'Nervous?' he asks, giving me a little squeeze. 'You've got nothing to be nervous about. Look at you.'

Ed opted for black jeans and a smart green shirt. He's rolled the sleeves up and done something to his hair which makes him look like the twenty-something man I fell in love with. I can't help but kiss him. This time away from the hustle and bustle of real life, the perma-fog of London that had curdled my brain, has done something to our relationship. I feel a renewed vigour for not only myself, but for Ed, too.

I take his hand and lead him to the door. The blast of sound and the sweet, fresh smell of alcohol mixed with expensive perfume hits us as Ed opens the door and ushers me through. Neither of us know anyone here, but it doesn't feel like the times when I was younger and I'd have to stand outside the pub waiting for my friends to arrive because I was too scared to go in on my own. Or the times it was raining and I couldn't wait outside because my hair would turn into Fizzgig and I'd pretend to be having a really in-depth text-versation with someone until my friends arrived. Or even the times in my own home, when I'd come downstairs to see what all the noise was, rubbing my eyes sleepily, waiting for Mum to come and tuck me back into bed, only to be told I didn't belong there and I'd have to drag my sleepy body back to bed and tuck myself in with Rabbity. No, this party has a calm, grown-up sense of belonging to it that doesn't include whispered jeers in the corners of rooms.

'I'll get us some drinks,' Ed says, his eyes searching for the bar.

'Thank you,' I say, pointing to where the sparkling optics have been decorated in garlands of bunting. 'Make it a double – for Pops.'

He gives me the cheeky grin that made me fall in love with him and heads off through the crowds. I take a moment to watch the people. Nick's mum has a lot of friends and they all look like people I'd want to be friends with, too. Their shiny, red-tinted faces look full of joy, and I'm positive it's not because of the free bar.

Then I spot Nick. He hasn't seen me yet; he's too busy talking to a young woman with the blondest hair I've seen and a dress that looks ethereal. Nick is wearing a black tuxedo with sharp lines, a crisp white shirt, and a bow tie. It adds to his loveable charm that he can dress so fine and still look so laid-back. He's got that casual lean going on, the one I saw him working at Mum's funeral, and the longer I watch him the more I start to recognise his date as the woman he was chatting up then, too. He is so easy with himself, so knowing of his body and his mind. He

146

looks approachable and open and she is putty in his hands once again. Unsurprisingly, seeing as he's a dad-finding, WD-40-wielding, party-for-his-mum organising, considerate man I have grown to know over the last few weeks.

Nick stops talking, his eyebrows creasing as his head cocks to the side, turning in my direction. He spots me. From the other side of the barn I see his sharp intake of breath and the widening of his eyes. And for a moment, so slight it may not actually be happening, it is as though we are the only two in the room. Lights flash around us, the music dulls to a quiet tune. I can hear the blood thumping in my ears as my heart rushes to my throat.

'Here you go.' It's Ed with a tall glass for me and a beer for himself. 'Isn't that Nick? Shall we go over and say hi?'

I tear my eyes away from Nick's to take my drink. It's cold to touch, the bubbles popping on the surface, spraying my hand, making me take notice. I smile at Ed.

'OK,' I say, letting him go first, trying to work out what on earth just happened.

The men shake hands and introduce themselves in that way men do when they don't really know each other. Ed grabs Nick's hand and brings him in for a hug, patting him hard on the back three times.

'Great party, Nick,' I hear him say as Nick watches me over Ed's shoulder. 'Thanks for the invite.'

Nick looks away from me briefly to Ed.

'Anything to keep Maggie smiling,' he says, his eyes darting back to mine.

He guides Ed out of his way with the gentle movement of an arm on his shoulder. And then he's there. Right in front of me.

'Margaret Burnett,' he says, his eyes bright, 'you look beautiful.'

And he kisses each of my cheeks and my skin ripples with goosebumps.

'Thanks,' I whisper as Ed slips an arm around my waist.

'This is Susie,' Nick says, stepping back in line with his date. 'Susie, this is Maggie and Ed.'

The pretty blonde with the amazing dress waves coquettishly at me and slips her own arm through Nick's. He kisses the top of her head. They look good together. Like people used to say about Ed and me. And all thoughts of the *moment* that I had felt Nick and I shared fly out the giant window we are all standing in front of. I wrap my arms around Ed and feel like I've arrived home. Ed and me. Me and Ed. And I'm still waiting for the awkward fizzle between Nick and me to peter out when he grabs my elbow and excuses us from our respective dates.

'I must just introduce you to my mum; she wants to say thanks for the flowers,' he gives me by way of excuse.

I bend my head around to mouth *sorry* to Ed but he is already busily talking to Susie.

Nick's mum looks everything I thought she would. Reminiscent of the forty-something I met once, dropping off homework, but different, too. Her long, grey hair falls down her back in ringlets and she's wearing a tea dress, bright colours, beautiful – and totally quirky. There is a man standing with her, suited and booted and the spitting image of Nick if he had been dehydrated like a prune.

'Mum,' Nick says, bouncing with energy, 'this is Maggie.'

The older woman looks at me with brilliant blue eyes and a wry smile.

'Hello, Maggie, it's so nice to meet you. Thank you for the beautiful flowers and please feel welcome in our home anytime you're nearby. Nick has talked non-stop about you since you returned to Norfolk.' She takes my hands in hers and studies my face. 'Don't you look like your mum!'

'You knew my mum?' I ask, the thought stealing my mind away from the fact that Nick has been talking to his mum about me.

She nods.

'You were right, Nick.' She turns back to her son and takes his face in her hands, kissing him on both cheeks as he had done to me moments earlier. 'She's lovely.'

Nick gathers his mum up in a hug. I look back over towards Ed as he waves at me and I feel tears prick my eyes at the look of love on his face. And, just like that, I feel part of something much bigger than me. A happy feeling of being wanted. Belonging. A family of sorts. Made up of friends and extended friends and, of course, Ed.

Chapter Twenty-Six

Happy birthday, dear Ivy, Happy birthday toooo yooooou.

Everyone cheers and holds up their glasses in good health to Ivy who looks glowing. There is a chant of *speech* that spreads around the room like a Mexican wave and she holds up her hand to quieten her waiting listeners.

'Thank you, thank you,' she starts, addressing the whole room which is now hushed to a pin-drop silence. 'I want to begin by taking the time to thank my husband.'

A loud cheer roars around the room and Nick's dad lifts an awkward hand and waves. Nick puts an arm around his dad's shoulders and hugs him tight, whispering something into his ear that makes his face light up.

'I'd also like to thank my son, Nick.' An even louder cheer fills the room, this time at a higher pitch than the last one. Susie takes Nick's free arm and holds on to it, her face slightly pinched as she tries to smile. 'He's been my rock over the last year, moving back home to help me look after his dad, giving up his time to look after *me*. His work with the at-risk families in Norfolk was his life and to put that to the side for the benefit of his family just shows how well I brought him up.'

A smattering of laughter fills the room, and Nick's mum's eyes sparkle with tears. My heart is overflowing with emotion at what Nick has done for his family. *That's* really why he's not been at work, and that's why he needed to make her party as money-efficient as possible. He's got so much on his plate, yet he's still making time to help me find my dad; really, he's a saint.

Ivy Forster is still talking as Nick's date, Susie, walks over and taps my arm.

'Is your dress supposed to be retro?' she whispers over the speech. 'Only it looks straight out of the eighties.' Her smile is frosty. 'It's nice that you've matched your hair to the decade, too. It's so . . . big.'

I pat my hair down. It *is* big. The heat always makes my hair expand and the barn is hot with bodies. She folds her well-manicured hands together and smiles saccharinely at me. Nick looks at us both and blows Susie a kiss. Her smile at me grows bigger. I shake my giant hair and lean my head against Ed's broad shoulder. Nick catches my eye and mouths to me *are you OK?* I nod, tucking my hair behind my ear in case he can't see my face from behind it. An uncomfortable lump sits in my chest and no amount of gin and tonic can shift it down. Susie turns back to the speech, her face enraptured at what Mrs Forster is saying.

Was she really just being mean, or am I a little over-sensitive?

I decide to pull her up on it.

'This dress was my mum's,' I whisper to her. 'So, yes, it is from the eighties, an original – which is more than I can say for some other things around here.'

I fold my arms across my chest and smile sweetly at Susie's frown. I wonder if Nick and she are a couple. Surely he would have mentioned her to me, wouldn't he? Though we have talked little about our romantic relationships, save me moaning about Ed and Nick defending his own honour after I accused him of being a little over-enthusiastic when it came to the opposite sex. Maybe they *are* a couple. A proper couple who do things like walks on the beach and romantic dinners for two. She certainly looks good next to him now – even if she was just a massive cow to me. A thought blasts its way into my mind that I don't want Nick going out with someone who doesn't like me. I'm enjoying spending time with him and if I'm going to have to put up with snide comments and blatant unkindness then that might put a dampener on our newly rekindled friendship. Then I remember I will be going back to London and our friendship will probably fizzle out anyway, because it's not quite repaired enough yet to turn into something sustainable. And that thought makes me sad. It's only when Nick turns back to me that I realise I've been staring at him this whole time. He slips me a knowing half-smile and I slip him a half-smile back.

A rapturous applause sounds out as Nick's mum finishes her speech. Nick turns and wraps her up in a bear hug, grabbing his dad's arm and pulling him into the hug, too. They're a close family and it's so nice to watch the bond they have, but it has me wanting to ask Nick about the man he thinks might be my dad. I want to start searching now. I want a family to hug *me* close and make me feel part of a team all of my own.

With Nick's attention fully on his family, Susie sidles up and starts talking to Ed as though I'm not here. She's stroking his arm and laughing at all his almost-jokes. What it is I've done to annoy her I am not sure of yet, but it's plainly clear that there's something getting to her. I try not to let it get to me, too.

'Ed,' I hear her say, her voice like a sexy chipmunk, 'what is it you have in common with Maggie? Do you like old things, too?'

She laughs like a fairy princess and Ed raises an eyebrow. I wait to see how this pans out.

'She's only thirty-two,' he says, and I have to stifle a laugh at his misunderstanding. 'I think she looks amazing for her age.'

'Nick, what do you think?' Ed says, nodding his head behind me. I turn and see Nick walking towards us. 'Maggie here looks good for her age, don't you think?'

I want the ground to open up and swallow me whole. I want Ed to just say I look good without the added bonus of *for my age*. I'm thirty-two, for Christ's sake, it's not as though I'm supposed to be old and shrivelled yet anyway. And I do *not* need Ed asking Nick what he thinks about my looks. It's demeaning, and I really don't think I want to know the answer, do I? From the looks of her mouth – which has turned the same shape as a cat's bumhole – Susie definitely *doesn't* want to know the answer to this either.

'Guys,' I say, lifting my arms up in a surrender of sorts, 'can we quit it with the demeaning comments already?'

I feel a bit closed-in while Ed and Susie study my face for the new wrinkles that are emerging as I stand here like a specimen. Nick walks round in front of me and blocks Ed and Susie from my view. Weirdly, he's closer than they were, but I feel less claustrophobic as he studies my face, relaxing as his eyes search mine. They're unwavering as he makes muttering noises of contemplation. My face radiates heat; they could all go grab some marshmallows and make s'mores with my cheeks. I can hear Susie huffing, but she's still blocked from my view by Nick's rather chiselled jaw. Ed is just laughing.

'I don't know how old you think she is, Susie,' Ed says from behind Nick, and I realise with the slurring of his words just how drunk he is, 'but she's amazing, is my Maggie. She's always been amazing. And she will be amazing when she's *actually* old, too.'

Susie scoffs.

'I didn't mean that. I don't think *she's* old. I was referring to her *clothes*. Do you like *vintage* things, *too*, Ed? That's what I meant, not, uh – oh, this is stupid. Come on Nick, let's go to the bar, I need a drink.' Susie is speaking but she could be miles away, her voice echoing around my ears. Nick moves closer to me, his breath warm on my face. It smells like expensive whisky and I like it.

My own breath catches in my throat. Goosebumps prickle all over my skin.

'I think you're beautiful,' he whispers, so quietly only I can hear him.

And for a split second the world stands still on its axis.

Chapter Twenty-Seven

It's the second time in a week I have arrived home to an unknown visitor in the house. The third time in a month if I count Ed's mistake, which I don't because I'm trying to put that out of my head.

Even from the taxi in the drive with a skinful of gin and a dash of tonic I can tell the place is lit up like Blackpool Illuminations. None of the curtains have been pulled shut and the windows are all open. If it's a burglar this time, then they have got it *all* wrong. And surely Pops wouldn't have left any lights on, let alone opened any of the windows? I pay the driver and nudge Ed with my elbow. He snorts awake.

'I wasn't asleep,' he protests, slurring his words as he opens his door and falls onto the shingle.

I walk ahead, still reeling at my own reaction to Susie. Since when do I care about what a young, pretty, intelligent woman thinks about me?

Since forever, actually, Mags. You've spent a lot of your life acting to impress others.

'Shut up, drunk brain,' I mutter under my breath as I open the door.

It pushes against something behind it, yielding only with my shoulder weighted against it. I step over a weekend bag and notice the two large suitcases blocking the way.

'Oh no! Oh no no no!' I say, as I recognise the Louis Vuitton logo splashed all over them. And, just like magic, I'm stone-cold sober.

'Maggie,' she says with a voice like the iceberg that sank the *Titanic*.

'Gwen, what are you doing here?' I reply, willing Ed not to throw up on the floor at her feet.

He is swaying so much that he'd probably projectile it over her luggage and that would be a fate worse than death. For Ed.

'Oh, bloody hell!' Ed leans forward and whispers in my ear at a rate of decibels that will get the neighbours complaining. His breath is one hundred per cent proof.

'Why don't you get to bed, Ed?' I say, patting him on the chest. 'I'll be right up.'

I pray silently that he is asleep before I make it up the stairs, because cuddling up to him would be like picking up a plastic beer glass that's already full to the brim and having to hold it tenderly so it doesn't spill over the top. He's so full, which hole the liquid will come squirting from is anyone's guess.

Ed doesn't argue with me; he utters a grunt of disgust in Gwen's face as he passes her and heads for the stairs. The grunt is so over the top and camp that I have difficulty in holding in my laughter. Which is much-needed after the disaster that was the end of the party.

After Nick had whispered about how beautiful I was right in my face, Susie had grabbed his arm and dragged him away from me. At one point his arm looked as though it was double-jointed – she's certainly strong, is Susie. Ed had spent a good half an hour raving about Susie's amazing achievements, by which time I had lost the will to live and tried to drown my sorrows in a lukewarm gin and tonic that wasn't going to top itself up. I had desperately wanted to talk to Nick about my dad. Or Nick's mum about how she knew my mum. But I knew I had to rein it in as the party was *not* about me and my issues.

'I had to come. And I'm glad I did because you're making a mess of Mum's house. If she could see what you have been doing, she'd be turning in her grave.'

Oh yes, Gwen's here.

'Mum's scattered over the North Sea off the coast of Cromer, Gwen. Hard to turn in your grave when you're not in one.' I can't help but be scathing back. I'm tired, still a little drunk, emotional from the party, emotional from the ups and downs of the search for my dad, *our* dad. I wonder for the first time if I should talk to Gwen about my search. But something stops me; it could be the look of pure hatred in Gwen's eyes.

'Don't talk about our mum like that. No wonder she couldn't stand being near you! You think you're so smart, think you're better than we are . . . were . . . Oh, whatever!' she spits at me.

I've never felt better than *anyone* in my whole entire life, that's not how I look at people. People are all different, there is no hierarchy of greatness, only a measure of human spirit. If anything, Gwen is the one who looks down on *me*. But the other bit of what she said, the part where Mum couldn't stand being anywhere near me, *that's* the truth. I've known it for years, but to hear my sister say it feels like a stab to the heart. A ball of pain lodges in my throat and tears prick my eyes.

We're still standing in the hallway; I haven't even had the chance to drop my bag and take off my jacket. Gwen has always had this knack of making me forget what I'm about to do because whenever we're together I have this sense of doom at what's to come. But maybe this is it, this is as bad as it's going to get. She's my sister, after all. Not my keeper. I start to shrug my jacket off my shoulders, hesitating at the last moment as I remember I'm wearing Mum's dress. Gwen pounces on my hesitations like a cheetah on a gazelle. Her eyes wander over my body, as though she can read my mind.

'You look like you're trying too hard to be the mum that didn't even like you.'

And with that she heads back to the kitchen to work on the rest of my demise. I feel an inch high. I should be used to it – it's not like Gwen has ever been my best friend. Well, not since we were old enough to make our own decisions. But it's never any easier to listen to someone who totally and utterly hates me. What happened to the innocent, childlike Gwen who used to take my hand and lead me to play? The Gwen who used to brush my hair with her own brush and chase me around the house, squealing with laughter as she caught me and tickled me? What did I do to make her hate me so much?

I trudge up the stairs, jacket and bag still on. Ed is snoring already; I can hear him from the landing and I now wish he was awake. I need him to tell me it'll be OK. I need to feel the warmth of kindness and compassion, because Gwen has sapped it all out of me in the matter of minutes we were talking. Her childhood bedroom door is open and I sneak a peek inside as I walk past. Another weekend bag sits proudly on her already made bed. How long is she staying for? I can't let her get in the way of Ed and me, or the search for Dad, but how can I do either of those if she's breathing down my neck?

Tiptoeing through to my own room so as not to wake Ed, I slip out of my jacket and Mum's dress. For a moment

I want to leave it lying in a pile on the floor. I thought it had looked good, but given the collective thoughts of Gwen and Susie I know otherwise. The pile of silky blue material looks accusingly at me and so I slip it over the hanger it came from and tuck it in my almost-empty wardrobe.

My phone beeps from the depths of my bag and I grab it and switch it to silent before lowering myself ever so slowly on the bed next to Ed. I may want a cuddle right now, but I can't wake a sleeping person just to get what I want.

Hope you're OK, didn't get to say goodbye. Thanks so much for everything you did to help. Mum loved the flowers. I'll message you tomorrow about your dad. Think I might be too drunk to type anymore. Maybe I can come over? Nick x

I smile.

My pleasure. Thank you too. We might need to find a new place to meet though. Gwen has turned up.

I make myself comfortable and can already feel the stress evaporating with the anticipation of what Nick might say.

Shocked face! Oh no, not the wicked witch of the east? Can you chuck a bucket of water over her and be done with it? Seriously though, Mags, don't forget, you have as much right to be there as she does. As much right to breathe the air as she does. And you are not just the components of her ideas of you. Stay strong, Burnett. Nx

He's right. What a night. I put my phone onto the little bedside table, warmth enveloping me as I cuddle the duvet around my neck.

Just as sleep is gathering me up in its arms, there's an almighty crash from downstairs. It's a proper crash, with the tinkling of broken glass and everything. Then Gwen starts screaming and I throw myself out of bed, grabbing my dressing gown from the back of the door and hurtle down the stairs to see if she's OK. Because although she may hate me and make me feel worthless, she's still my sister.

Bien que je sois à l'autre bout du monde, mon cœur est toujours avec vous. Cher E, écoute l'océan et ton cœur peut être avec moi aussi.

Though I'm on the other side of the world, my heart is always with you. Dear E, listen to the ocean and your heart can be with me, too.

Chapter Twenty-Eight

'What have you done?' Gwen screams at me from the mess in the kitchen.

It's as though a bomb has gone off. It's like the aftermath of a rampage of a very angry, very strong person who has taken their rage out on Mum's kitchen. I can make out the reason for the loud crash amongst the debris. The cupboard where Mum kept all her favourite crockery, a cupboard we were banned from even *looking* at is no longer attached to the wall. In fact, it *is* the debris. Pieces of flaked painted wood stick up at dangerous angles, some still attached to the glass from the doors that Gwen and I would sneak a peek through to see the plates that were more precious to our mum than we were. The plates are in shattered piles around Gwen's feet.

'Were you in the plate cupboard?' I ask, incredulously.

'No, I wasn't *in it*!' she spits back at me. 'I just wanted to have a look. All I did was open the door.'

'I didn't mean sitting in it, Gwen. I *meant* were you *looking* in it?' I laugh, I can't help it. The very idea of Gwen sitting in the cupboard sends me over the tired edge I've been walking.

'Shut up!' she hisses at me. 'Just shut up. What have you been doing to the cupboard to make it fall off the wall on top of me?'

'Gwen,' I say, trying to regain a little composure, 'I haven't even touched that bloody cupboard since I arrived here. We're not allowed, remember? And you, of all people, should know that.'

'Well then, why did it just fall on me? You must have done something to knock it loose. I can't move.'

I look at her bare feet, her toenails perfectly red which makes her fake tan look lovely. I curl up my own chipped nails and think about all the broken glass and china.

'Why were you looking in the cupboard? It's the middle of the night.'

'Just shut up about the cupboard and sort out this mess!'

There's no *please can you help me?* with Gwen, it's always a demand accompanied by a look that tells me I should have figured out what to do by now and done it already.

'I'll get the dustpan. Hold on, I'll need some shoes.'

I slink back out into the hallway and slip on a pair of trainers Ed has left by the door, clown footing it back to Gwen before she self-combusts.

'I wanted to check you'd not sold off any of the plates,' Gwen says as I'm rummaging around in the cupboard under the sink.

I don't stoop to her level with a reply. Carefully, I pick up the large pieces of cupboard and move them to the side. I'm too tired to clean up properly; that can wait until the morning. For now, I just need to get Gwen out without her losing a toe or chipping her nail varnish. I make a path through the glass and broken plates, brushing what I can from her feet, too. She takes some tentative steps towards me and her arms reach out. I think she's going to hug me, but I mistake her need for me to get out of her way as a sign of affection. She pushes me over a bit so she can stand where I was standing.

A wave of exhaustion floods me. I know there's not going to be a thanks coming, so I excuse myself and head back up to bed and a snoring Ed.

★

The morning brings with it a ray of sunshine streaming through the gap in my curtains and a headache to rival that time I fell off my bike onto the pavement outside my house.

'Ow,' I moan, sinking into the duvet, trying to hide my face from the sun.

I didn't think I had drunk that much. Wracking my brains to remember the previous night, it comes flooding back with a nauseous lurch. The party, Susie's foul words, Ed drinking his body weight in beer, Gwen.

Oh God, surely not.

That must have been a dream, right? Gwen wouldn't just show up here with her million Louis Vuitton bags and the touch of Thor. The cupboard. I drag the duvet over my head and think of the mess waiting for me down in the kitchen.

Ed groans at my movement. 'I had a nightmare that Gwenifer is here. Please tell me I dreamt it? Oh God, why did you let me drink so much? I feel sick.'

I drag myself out of bed and throw on some jogging bottoms and a T-shirt – my body hurts too much for underwear – and plod downstairs with my phone in my hand. I'm scrolling through Nick's messages to make sure I didn't write anything awful about what Susie said to me. I don't want to lose Nick's friendship over a girl. I'm pleased to see we had an amicable chat about the evening and then I remember my dad and my stomach lurches so much I think I actually am going to be sick. I need coffee and orange juice and something stodgy to soak up the gin. Then I'll message Nick and we can sort something out. The house feels quiet, as though I'm the only one here. Ed's snores have been soaked up by the thick walls and maybe I did dream Gwen coming home. She would be up already and chastising me for lying in past sunrise. I check the time on my phone and groan as it's only 7 a.m. Then I brace myself for the kitchen.

It's a miracle. There's no sign of the broken cupboard. The smashed plates are as forgotten about as they were when I arrived back home. I'm beginning to think that maybe I *did* imagine it, and if it wasn't for the massive great gap in the wall where the cupboard used to be, I would not believe it if I said Gwen was home.

Walking up to the space I stroke the rough plasterwork with a finger, just to make sure.

Nope, definitely not there anymore.

Pops is already out in the garden, so I take him an early coffee and perch on the rotten windowsill of the long-forgotten dining room. It's another sash window that needs replacing because the beetles have made themselves at home there. I push the thought to the side and watch Pops tend lovingly to a spindly green plant with pretty white flowers. He looks a bit more like himself today, less grey and sweaty.

'How was it, then?' he asks, leaning on his rake and sipping his coffee.

'Everyone loved your flowers, Pops.'

He smiles at me. 'Of course they did. And did your young man enjoy himself? Did him and Nick get on OK?' He has a wry smile on his face and I think he's teasing me. But there is no reason to tease me, is there?

'Yep, of course they did,' I say, shaking my head. 'No jealousy between my *boyfriend* and an old school friend who is helping me find my dad.'

I figure that's a good enough rudder to steer the conversation away from Pops' searching questions about Nick and Ed. I have no idea why he's so vested in my love life.

'Your dad?'

It's worked.

But Pops' face has greyed and he stands upright from the rake.

'Yes,' I say, finishing up my coffee to hide my reddening face. 'Nick thinks he may have found something out about my dad so we're going on a manhunt. I'm a bit nervous but I really want to find out about him. Especially now I have no one left.'

Pops looks on the verge of saying something. Probably about to tell me that I still have Gwen. Gwen!

'Oh yes, and Pops, just as a warning . . .' I am about to tell him about my sister coming to stay when her screeching tones supersede me.

'About time you're awake. I had to sort the kitchen out all by myself. I don't appreciate still being left to fix the things you seem intent on breaking all the time. I may be your older sister, but you're a grown-up and should be able to act like one.' She jogs up to us, her hair fixed in a ponytail, her face free of makeup and looking surprisingly young without her slick of dark lipstick and even darker eyeshadow. I'm so stunned by how amazingly fit her body looks in Lycra that I kind of ignore how she just blamed me for taking a cupboard I haven't touched for at least twenty years off the wall.

'Gwen's here,' I shrug at Pops as he raises an eyebrow at me.

'Ah, the gardener,' Gwen says, looking him up and down.

'Maggie,' Pops takes my arm, 'about what you were just saying—'

'No time for that now,' Gwen says, dragging my arm away from Pops and towards her. 'We have some cleaning to do.'

I think of the kitchen and the floor that is already so clean I could eat my breakfast from it if I wasn't feeling too hungover to get down so low.

'Gwen,' I start to say – I don't want her being rude to Pops – but she's already dragging me away.

'Sorry!' I shout to Pops as Gwen hoists me in through the patio doors to the sparkly clean kitchen.

Pops scratches his chin with his free hand as he watches. There's something about the look on his face that makes me really curious about what he was going to say. But the thoughts are soon swept from my head as Gwen slides the kitchen doors closed and turns to face me.

'Stop inviting all these weirdos to our house!' she spits in a hushed voice. 'First, that old man who does nothing for a garden that wants ripping out – I'm going to lay artificial grass at the soonest opportunity so the house will sell. Then your weird friends who came over and drank all of Mum's alcohol and ate at my table. And that *boy* we went to school with who was always stuck in the library because he had no friends. Does Ed know how often he's been here? Or what you've been getting up to with him?'

I hold up my hand to stop her mid-speech. But I can see Ed over her shoulder and his face drops as he overhears Gwen's tirade.

'What? What *have* you been getting up to with him?' Ed asks, before I have the chance to stop her.

'Nothing,' I say, holding my hands up in defence. 'Only what I've already told you, Ed.'

Gwen scoffs and we both turn to look at her. She's swishing her ponytail around, her nose right in the air.

'So you've told him everything, have you?' she says, batting her eyelashes at Ed. 'I'll bet!'

It's Ed's turn to scoff now.

'And I suppose she's told *you* exactly what she and Nick are looking for, hasn't she? As the two of you are so close?'

'Ed, don't,' I warn him. I have told him how important it is to me that *I* find my father, not Gwen. Gwen knowing about this would ruin everything.

'What's that supposed to mean?' Gwen gets closer to Ed, her toes near the tip of his. It's as though I'm not even here.

'Oh, she hasn't?' Ed says, nodding in Gwen's face. 'She's not told you she found a load of old letters and now Nick is helping her find your dad?'

Gwen's open but quiet mouth tells Ed everything he needs to know. And I walk out of the room, slamming the door behind me.

Chapter Twenty-Nine

'He *what*?!' Perdita yells, choking on the handful of fries she's just stuffed in her mouth.

'Shit, Mags,' Phillip adds, his own hands dripping with burger juice, 'no sexual favours for at least a month.'

I snort. My burger and fries sit cold on the grass beside me. Whoever suggested that a McDonald's could cheer me up was very much mistaken. The thought of greasy fries and a burger that will sit in my stomach alongside hunger, because it has no nutritional value, makes me want to heave. A KFC, on the other hand . . .

I pick at the grass, listening to the kids playing in the play area at the other end of the park with not a care in the world except that they get to have a turn on the swing or a go on the slide. My hangover is subsiding, though Phillip's driving did not help my nausea. I didn't moan too much though, as he did come and pick me up and drive me to Norwich at the first sign of an SOS text. Perdita suggested the park and I didn't have the brain space to think of anywhere I'd rather be.

'I think this might be more than refusing to ride him like a cowgirl, Phillip,' I say, grimacing. 'Though that would be a shame, because he's got this thing he does—'

Phillip holds up his hands, his burger flopping dangerously close to his shirt.

'Not while I'm eating!' he yells.

'He's broken my trust again,' I say, not looking up from the bit of grass I am maiming. 'Though I know how frustrating Gwen can be – she used to make me blow my fuse all the time too. And I've had longer to learn to curb my anger. And I suppose I *have* been seeing a lot of Nick.'

Perdita coughs.

'He's helping me find my dad!' I say exasperatedly. 'Plus, he has a girlfriend now anyway. Plus I LOVE ED!'

'Anyway, it's not as if Ed has a leg to stand on, is it?' Phillip adds.

'No!' Perdita agrees. 'Besides, you can spend as long as you like with friends, if you're sure that's all it is. Ed never gets jealous over you spending time with Phillip, does he? And even if Ed had three legs to stand on – which from all accounts he does – he still had no right to get annoyed enough with you to go against your wishes like that. No, he has a lot of making up to do.'

We all fall into a silence. They're right, my friends, as always.

'Are you sure that's all it is with Nick, Mags?' Perdita asks, going back to her chips. 'Friends? You just have this way about you when you're talking about him.'

Lying back down on the grass so I don't have to show them my blushing cheeks, I think about it. I think about the way he has been there for me recently. The way he looked when he caught sight of me at the party. The way he told me I'm beautiful. But more than that: the way he makes me feel about myself.

'Urgh,' I sigh, looking up at the bright blue sky. There are no clouds as far as my eyes can see. 'Honestly, I don't know any more. I'm so confused. What about Ed? He's trying really hard to make it up to me. *Was* trying. We have a house and a life together. I can't just throw that away for a boy I used to fancy who HAS A GIRLFRIEND. But what Ed did just now brought back all those feelings of mistrust; what if that's always going to be my default feeling when it comes to Ed now?'

Phillip strokes my hair, hopefully with his non-burger hand.

'Maybe you need to go and talk to Ed, rather than us? Sort through these feelings with him. Has he messaged you?'

I shrug, which is hard to do lying down, and pull out my phone.

I'm so sorry, Mags, it's your sister. She's so frustrating in her need to be right all the time. I shouldn't have let her get to me. I'm sorry I told her. I didn't mean to, it just came out. Please come back so we can talk. Gwen is avoiding me and she hasn't mentioned your dad at all. I'm sorry. I love you. x

I go to reply to him but another message pings through.

Can you get to my office in the city today? It's Gwen-free and I've got something to show you. Nick.

I scrunch up my eyebrows. It's almost as though the universe is testing me. Home to Ed, or away with Nick? But it's not just Nick, it's my dad. And Ed will understand. I send a quick reply to Nick, asking for his office address, and leave Ed's message unanswered. A weighty feeling sits in my stomach and I can't blame the food. I sit up and think about telling my friends that I've just ignored Ed and am going to meet Nick instead, but I'm too ashamed.

'Right, losers,' Perdita says, slapping her hands on her knees, 'I've got to love you and leave you. I have a date this evening and my nether regions are in need of a wax.'

Phillip and I snigger.

'Who's the lucky recipient of your smooth feefee?' Phillip asks.

'You may have a child, Phillip, but that's no reason not to call a vagina a vagina. Tell your daughter young enough and she won't be too embarrassed to say it loud and proud when she's older.' Perdita starts shouting the word around the park, much to the scorn of the yummy mummies in the play area. She turns her attention back to us. 'I went to see my chiropractor a few weeks ago to sort out my spine – it hurts being on your feet for hours on end, even in flats. Anyway, when I got there my usual worker, Tiff, was off with the squits and I was faced with a fit young man with *the* cutest smile. I was glad I'd worn my best active wear for the occasion, because normally I wear my old joggers and that would never have done.

'So I was lying there, face down on the table, waiting for him to get in there with his elbows and crack my back into submission, and then he just whipped down not only my leggings but my knickers, too. I just thought I'd got lucky so I flipped over onto my back and whipped his trousers down as well. Turns out he was about to jab me with acupuncture needles and not his cock. Still, it turned out OK in the end and we're off out for a proper date this evening.'

'It's called a penis, Perdita,' Phillip says, a wry smile on his face.

'And you are being one!' she replies, kissing us on the cheeks and jogging away to her appointment.

'Do you want a lift home?' Phillip asks, getting to his feet and brushing the grass from his shorts. 'I've got to head back now anyway – we're off to the beach for fish and chips this afternoon. Don't know how I'm going to fit it all in.'

He rubs his flat stomach with both hands and I raise an eyebrow at him.

'No thanks, Phillip, I think I'll get the train. I quite fancy a mooch around the shops,' I say, following his lead out of the park. 'Thanks for today, though, I really appreciate it.'

'No probs, Mags.' He hugs me close and I feel safe. 'Take care of yourself, OK? And if you need to talk through how you're feeling, I'm just at the end of the phone. Unless you want to come to the beach with us?'

'No,' I say, not wanting to sound ungrateful but I have just heard my phone go in my bag and I'm hoping it's Nick. 'You go and have time with your family. I'll be OK.'

We hug again and he heads off to the car park. I wait a few moments then look at the address of Nick's office. And with my stomach churning once again, I head to the old cobbled roads in the medieval part of the city.

N. Forster Associates is written in clear print on the unobtrusive sign above the door. The building is wonky, like its neighbours; they're all holding each other up because seventeenth-century workmen can't have heard of spirit levels. Nick's office sits between a wattle-and-daub estate agents advertising properties of my dreams and a Tudor-clad solicitors. His own office is single storey, sitting pretty with black beams and a door I have to duck to get through. Inside is cool, in more ways than one. Modern fittings belie the exterior and a huge iMac takes up most of the desk. It's just a single room with a door at the back. But there's no sign of Nick.

'Hello,' I shout tentatively, 'is there anyone there?'

I feel as though I'm in an episode of *Midsomer Murders*. The whole office has that quaint, quirky feeling and if I go and open the door at the back of the room the dead body of a vicar will fall on top of me from a cupboard. I perch on the edge of one of the comfy chairs by the window and watch people go by, hoping I didn't get Nick's invite totally wrong. There are a few magazines scattered on the low table by the chairs and I flick through a new copy of *National Geographic*, marvelling at how brilliant some photographers are and how I am just pleased that iPhone now have a portrait mode that make my pictures look presentable. I like Nick's office. It's calm and ordered and wouldn't make me feel intimidated if I was here because I needed his help with a family law matter. Which makes sense as I do need his help with a family matter, and I am feeling calm.

'Maggie,' Nick says, coming through the door at the back of the office, with not a dead body in sight, 'I'm so sorry, have you been waiting long?'

Nick in work clothes is enough to render me speechless. Without his suit jacket, long-forgotten on the back of his office chair, he looks grown-up and in charge in an expensive-looking shirt and tie. His sleeves are rolled up, giving me another great view of his forearms. I open my mouth to reply but no words come out.

'I was just, uh, making a private call.' He holds up his mobile and looks sheepish.

'Susie?' My voice has returned.

Nick looks questioningly at me and comes to sit on the comfy chair next to me. He smells amazing.

'Susie and me, we're complicated.'

'Look, Nick,' I say before he goes into details that I don't want to hear because I think they'll make me feel jealous, 'it's really none of my business what you get up to in your private life. Susie, Sarah, Sammy, Steve — it's all good.'

Now I really don't know what I'm saying because it's all a great big jumble in my head. There's no clarity anymore. Ed, my true love who may have broken my trust but who is worth fighting for because he is what I know and is who I love. Yet I'm sitting here with Nick whose heart I probably broke years ago, who seems to have taken up residence in my head. But I *am* thinking about it. I am wondering what it would be like to kiss those soft lips, to have his manly hands run over my body and through my hair. Am I just having these thoughts about Nick because I want to get back at Ed? Do I want Nick? Or do I just want the revenge?

'Maggie?'

I recover my thoughts quick enough to bring myself back into Nick's office.

'So let's get started on the search for my dad,' I say, as Nick looks like he's about to talk to me more about Susie. 'That's why you asked me here, isn't it?'

He runs his hands through his hair and gets up, going over to his desk.

'OK,' he says, huffing out air through his pursed lips, 'come over here and bring that chair round.'

I do as he says, making sure I leave enough space so our legs aren't touching each other. A picture of his mum and dad covers the large screen of his computer and my insides melt a little further.

'So what have we got?' I ask, careful not to look directly at him.

He moves the mouse a little and opens up his emails. I watch his hands, trying desperately to think about how much I love Ed. Dragging my eyes to the screen instead, I see that Nick has no unread emails. How is that even possible? I thought *everyone* had thousands of unread emails like I do. The sight is amazing and I want to ask him about it, but he's clicked open a folder marked 'private' and moves the mouse to a folder inside that with my name on it which opens to show only a couple of emails sorted there.

'This was the email I received from my friend. The wedding certificate is scanned onto it, so see what you think.'

He clicks on it and a faded yellow certificate fills the screen. I lean in, thoughts of Nick and Ed long gone as I see my mum's name written in blue ink and above it, as plain as day, Leonard Simpson. My dad.

'Oh my God, Nick!' I say, turning to him and completely forgetting the distance I was trying to keep between us. 'This is *amazing*. Thank you so much.'

I lean over to hug him in my excitement, my chair sliding easily on its castors. His arms wrap around me, his bare arms hot through the back of my dress. My skin breaks out in goosebumps as it tickles from his touch. I draw my head back a bit, our arms still wrapped around each other. Our faces are so close together that our lips are almost touching. I can't move. His eyes darken as they find mine, his breath sounds ragged and my own isn't much better.

My phone vibrates in my bag.

Ed.

I move back, dropping my arms from around Nick's neck. My face is throbbing with heat. Nick pushes his chair away from the desk with his arms and clears his throat. I reach down into my bag, as much to hide my face as anything else. It's just Phillip checking I'm OK. I puff out air and sit upright again, brushing my hair out of my face. The heat from my cheeks has it doubling in size.

'So, where do we go from here?' I ask.

Chapter Thirty

'So, you and Nick met up in Norwich today? That's nice.' Ed looks pointedly at Gwen at the kitchen table over the stew I have made too much of because I want to give some to Pops next time I see him – he's looking a bit thin.

'Yes, he had some things we needed to go over.' I'm not going to go into detail and part of me wishes Ed had not brought it up just so he could make a point about his indifference to Gwen. Gwen pokes baby carrots around with her fork and looks as if she's been asked to eat a favourite family pet and not chicken from Sainsburys. 'I spent most of the day with Perdita and Phillip, though. We went and sat in the park, it was lovely.'

Gwen scoffs but her thoughts stay unspoken. The tension around the table is so taut it could be cut with the blunt knives my mum has had since before I was born that Gwen is finding so difficult to use this evening. We pick at our food, Gwen and I, and Ed scoffs his down as though he's not sitting in the middle of what could be the start of a Burnett civil war. Rain is pattering at the window, the first rain since I've moved back home and in the back of my mind I'm wondering where the drips will start to soak the carpets first.

'I know you wanted to make something for the old man that enjoys hanging around our garden, Margaret, but you could have put some sort of seasoning in it, it won't kill him, you know.'

I chew a piece of chicken so ferociously that it ends up disintegrated in my mouth before I can swallow. It probably wouldn't get past the lingering anger clogging up my throat anyway.

'And after dinner,' Gwen is still speaking, 'we're all going to start filling rubbish bags with Mum's things so we can get the house ready to put on the market. I don't need a money pit like this weighing me down.'

Ed's fork stops halfway to his mouth. A blob of gravy falls onto his shirt.

'You are selling, then?' he asks her.

'We haven't actually discussed what we're doing with the house yet, Ed,' I say forcefully.

My anger is directed at the wrong person, I know this, but I find it so hard to stand up to my big sister because everything that comes out of her mouth directed at me chips me down. It has done for years and so I don't have any steel left to stand up to her.

'I think selling would be a good—' he starts, but Gwen interjects.

'It's no business of yours what we do with the house, Edwin. So, keep your nose out and just help us fill the bin bags. God knows there will be enough rubbish to keep us all busy for the next few days.'

Ed shifts in his seat and I can see he's giving me the side-eye. I don't want to look.

'Um,' he says, and I can hear his excuse building as loudly as his brain cogs whirring, 'I can't stay for much longer. I have to get back to work.'

What?

'Well, make yourself useful while you're still here and

clear away these dishes. Obviously we're all feeling the lack of taste of this awful stew.'

Ed does as Gwen tells him and I sit quietly and seethe.

'I thought the stew was nice,' I pipe up eventually, sick of chewing my cheeks. 'I just lost my appetite when you started making claims to a property that isn't wholly yours.'

'What do *you* know about property?' Gwen asks. 'You live in a godawful flat that you don't even own.'

Ed starts clattering the dishes together around us and I hope he splatters bits of stew gravy on Gwen's stupid head.

'I know enough to know that we own half each and I'm not sure I want to sell the place.' Now I've said it I realise it might be true.

Gwen laughs in my face.

'What are you going to do? Live here?'

'Maybe, I don't know yet.'

'What about me? What about your job?' Ed asks

'What about the fact you were never happy here?' Gwen asks at the same time.

I push my chair out from under the table and place both hands on the wood in front of me.

'Both of you can just leave me alone for a moment. I'm going to pack up the rest of the food for Pops – at least *he* appreciates me.'

'Takes advantage of you, you mean!' Gwen shouts from her seat as I storm over to the cooker and rummage around noisily for a Tupperware large enough to fit the leftovers in.

Ed comes over to me and places his hand on the large Bolognese stained tub I clatter on the counter. He whispers so Gwen can't hear from her seat at the head of the table.

'Do you really want to stay here?' he asks me. 'I thought we were going to sort things out between us. I really think we are OK. You could sell up and we could buy a place together with your money. Christ, we could pay off our debts with what your Mum has in her savings account which is now technically yours. Don't stay here. I want us to be together.'

'What about you?' I say, dolloping stew into the tub. 'You're leaving right now? I thought you had a few weeks off work. *I* thought we were going to sort stuff out.'

'I can't stay here with *her.*' He nods his head towards my sister, but he needn't have because I knew who he was talking about, and I honestly can't say I blame him.

'But you can't leave me here on my own with her either, can you?'

Ed takes his hands off the plastic pot and places them on my cheeks.

'I love you, Mags,' he says, kissing my nose. 'But I cannot do anything at all with her near me.'

'Urgh, get a room,' Gwen shouts across the kitchen. 'Ed, get the bin bags, we can start in the living room.'

I click the lid on Pops' stew and put it in the fridge, wishing I could shut my head in there, too, just to get away for a few quiet minutes. Still, at least Gwen didn't suggest Mum's room, where the remnants of Mum's wedding dress are still scattered on the floor, or the study, where the paperwork I'm sorting through is strewn on the desk.

My phone beeps as I'm mustering the strength to tackle Mum's things with Gwen breathing down my neck. Gwen and Ed are already bickering in the other room, so I take a moment to sit quietly at the table and read my message.

We may have hit a snag, have you got time to talk? Can I come over? Nick.

My stomach sinks a notch lower.

Not right now. Not a good time. Tomorrow?

I'm away on holiday with Susie for a few days.

I thought my stomach had reached rock bottom, but I was wrong. Nick's name flashes up on my screen as he calls me. I hit the green button and answer him.

'Maggie, sorry, I thought it would be easier to call than to text everything I have found.'

'That's OK, it's nice to hear your voice.' I step out into the garden and slide the door shut silently behind me, grateful again for Nick's handyman skills. 'What's happened?'

I can hear him moving around and then a rush of traffic beside him. 'Look, Mags,' he says in a hushed voice, 'I've been doing some digging on Leonard Simpson and I'm not sure about what I've found.'

I prepare myself for the worst.

'Oh God,' I say, leaning against the crumbling window-sill so I don't collapse. 'He's in jail, isn't he? That's why I've never met him! What's he in for? Come on, do your worst, Nick. Unless it's something to do with children, then I really don't think I want to know. Is it something to do with children?'

I grimace.

'What? No, Maggie, that's not it at all.'

'Then he's dead,' I blurt. 'He died years ago and Mum never told me because she didn't care that I would end up searching for him.'

A very loud bus horn blasts over the phone and an angry bike bell follows. Nick apologises and we wait for quiet to settle so I can hear what he's saying.

'Maggie, shut up for just a moment and let me finish, please. I've only got a few minutes before I have to go.'

Off on holiday with Susie.

'OK, sorry,' I say.

'I thought that something about the dates and names didn't add up. And at first I couldn't work it out, so I did some digging on the name we thought was your dad, LS. Then it hit me, your last name, Burnett. That wasn't your dad's last name and normally kids take their father's name, don't they?'

'Yes, but I don't think Mum would have done that,' I say, interrupting Nick because he doesn't really know what Mum was like and I don't want this to not be real. I want to find my dad. 'Gwen and I always had Burnett as a surname, so did Mum. It was her parents' married name. She never took Dad's name so Leonard not being a Burnett would be OK.'

I feel relieved that Nick's bout of disbelief was nothing to worry about. What with Gwen arriving home and Ed about to leave me alone with her, the last thing I need right now is a spanner in the works of the only good news I have left.

'No, sorry, Maggie, that wasn't it,' Nick continues. 'I started looking into Leonard because of my concern over the name, but when I found the Leonard who is mentioned on the wedding certificate he is still living in Yorkshire and is still married to Elizabeth. So, it can't be your dad, can it? Because *that* Elizabeth isn't your mum.'

I feel the air deflate out of my body with such force that my knees feel wobbly.

'Sorry, Maggie, I've got to go, Susie is waving me from the office window. I'll message when I can, but I wanted to let you know what I'd found.' I can hear the little bell above the door tinkle as he walks back inside and Susie's chipmunk voice asks him who he's talking to. 'Don't worry. It's not the end of the search. It's just a crossed-off avenue, that's all. Take care. Speak soon.'

He hangs up and I let the phone fall by my side. I had been so certain that Leonard was my dad that I had been looking for him on the ancestry website, using my free searches, imagining what he looks like and how it would be the first time we meet. And now all I'm left with is a sad sense of longing for everything that is falling around beside me.

There is a tap at the window behind me and I turn to see Ed's questioning face as he holds up a half-full black bin bag. He must have wandered into the dining room at some point during my conversation and I speculate on how much he overheard.

Quand tout semble perdu, chérie E, n'oublie jamais que toi et moi sommes ce qui compte. Je serai bientôt à la maison. LS

When all seems lost, darling E, never forget that you and I are what matters. I'll be home soon. LS

Chapter Thirty-One

I wake early the next morning and tiptoe downstairs. The house creaks loudly around me and I will with all my might that it doesn't wake Ed or Gwen. I need a moment's peace, some time to myself to think over the roller coaster of the week. And to tidy away the paperwork in Mum's old office. Gwen had been ruthless last night. The living room looked as naked as my room had when she'd finished throwing away all of Mum's memories. No photos of Mum up anymore, no stacks of papers and magazines, no dying plants. Gwen had scooped them all up with her sidekick, Ed, and lined the hallway with full sacks to take to the tip. I'd managed to sneak a couple of plants I thought I might be able to revive and took them up to my room with the pretence of giving them to Pops. The withering look that Gwen had given me was almost as bad as the enthusiastic encouragement from Ed.

It was as though he was being too nice. His arms had reached out for a hug when I'd skimmed over the conversation I'd had with Nick. Encouraging words had spilled from his mouth, yet I could feel the desperation in the tightness of the hug and the over-the-top way he was positive about still finding my dad. It's almost as if he is scared of losing me. Which is a crazy fear. Ed was the one who had cheated, not me; surely I should be the one with trust issues? But at the moment all I have is an overwhelming sense of numbness at it all.

The office is gloomy this early in the morning. I throw back the heavy curtains and cough at the dust, adding dry cleaning to my list of things to do to the house to make it liveable. Rain is still pattering at the window as I push it up, bringing with it a welcome breeze and the feeling of the impending autumn. I'll have to return to London soon and get back to work, if they ever get back in contact with me with a date I'm allowed to grace them with my presence.

Maybe it's what I need. To get away from this place again, back to normality, back to my own life. A life that I forged so hard to achieve, one where I am free to just get on with things. A world away from feeling the way I felt growing up here. Maybe the sense of dread I'm feeling now isn't to do with a dad who may or may not exist, or Gwen, or Ed leaving me alone with Gwen, or even Nick jetting off somewhere hot and exotic with sour-faced Susie. Maybe it's just the memories of not feeling wanted soaking back into my skin after being back home for so long.

I lump down into the desk chair and start making piles with the paperwork that I'd stacked on the desk. One pile for my eyes only. One pile for Gwen to throw away as though our mother had loved me more than her and not the other way around. The love letters from the dress I put carefully in the front pocket of my dungarees again, so if Gwen decides to come in here now to check up on me, at least she won't see them. Not once do I feel guilty for doing so. Gwen has a heart of ice; she wouldn't care that Dad wrote Mum the cutest love letters and that Mum had sewn them into her dress because she once had feelings that didn't need to be triggered by alcohol.

The dusty pile of old newspapers and bills is ready and waiting for Gwen to do her worst. There are a few bits and bobs for me to save – solicitors' letters, that sort of thing. I'll keep them safe and show them to Gwen once she's over this need to Marie Kondo the shit out of our family home.

The house is stirring. Ed must be getting up. I brush my hands down and get up from the desk to go and see him. He looks like he hasn't slept properly, though when I left him he was snoring contently. His eyelids look like they're weighed down by an invisible hook, or a worry – that's more likely.

'Morning,' I say, and I go over to where he's filling the kettle and give him a kiss.

'You're up early?'

'Yeah, I wanted to sort some paperwork before Gwen bins it all,' I say, popping some bread in the toaster.

'Oh,' he almost sighs with relief. 'Yes, that makes sense, your mum does have so much of it and you'll need all her bank statements and things, won't you? Don't want Gwen throwing away your inheritance. I had wondered if you were doing some more searching for your dad. With Nick.'

I keep my eyes on the toaster.

'No, Nick's away for a few days with Susie. I'm going to concentrate on the house while he's away so Gwen can't get her own way and tear the place down.'

'Look, Maggie.' He hands me a cup of milky tea. 'I've been thinking about Gwen wanting to sell this place.'

We sit down at the table and I silently eat my toast as Ed talks about his wishes for my house.

'It's not like you've got any money to do the place up. It's leaky and draughty and it's getting close to winter. Plus, do you really want to be reminded of your childhood all day every day? You used to tell me how glad you were to get away from the place. I mean, don't get me wrong, it could be beautiful, for someone who has the time and money to do up an old Georgian rectory. But that's not *us,* is it, Mags? We can barely afford our own rent, let alone bills and council tax for a beast like this. But if you sell up, we can pay off all our debts, buy a place to call our own, make a proper fresh start in London where we know people and where our jobs are.'

I take another bite of buttery toast so I can think about what he's just said before I answer. Because he's the one who ran up the debt, he's the one who loves his job. But I know he's right. I don't want to stay here and be reminded of my failure to be a loving daughter every day. I need to get back to London fast.

'Maybe I should come back with you when you go?'

'No, I think you need to stay here and look after your inheritance in case Gwen decides she's more worthy. Which isn't beyond her, is it? In fact, I'd be surprised if she hasn't already found the will and doctored it to pass everything down to the eldest, like the throne she likes to put herself on.'

'The solicitor already has the will; he did the reading a while ago and we know it's split equally already,' I say frowning, wiping butter from my chin with the back of my hand.

'Well, anyway. I'll head back to London in the next couple of days and you can come back in a few weeks when your job starts again. It'll go quickly, you'll see,' he adds, when he sees my grimace. 'Talk of the devil.'

Gwen bursts in through the kitchen doors, a slight sheen on her glowing skin. She stretches out her calves on the threshold step and Ed's eyes flicker almost imperceptibly to her taut backside flaunted in tight running shorts. A sickening wave of jealousy hits me in the stomach and I take another mouthful of thick, buttered toast to wash it down.

He hates Gwen, don't be an idiot.

'We're going to sort out the rest of the rubbish from downstairs today. I hope you're actually going to pull your weight this time, Margaret. God knows there's enough of it and no wonder if you're going to eat that crap for breakfast. It's disgusting.'

Ed starts to say something but is shut down quickly by Gwen.

'And you're not much better, Ed. You could do with a little more exercise, too. Though I'm glad you're not filling your body with fats and carbs like my sister.'

'What?' he says, wrapping his arms around his T-shirted waist to protect his stomach from Gwen but she doesn't notice, she's too busy waltzing out of the kitchen wafting with her the scent of righteousness and Paco Rabanne and not even a hint of sweat which is totally unfair.

'Were you looking at her bum?' I ask, pushing my plate to the side, the toast's appeal long gone, the butter starting to congeal on the cold china.

'Why are you asking me that? Out of all the things your sister has just said to us, you pick that to say to me!' He sounds defensive and my mind starts whirring.

'Right.' I don't know what else to say. Am I wrong in feeling anxious? Is this feeling of uncertainty going to cut through every thought from now on because Ed couldn't keep it in his pants? Is this how betrayal really ends relationships? Not the shock of the act but the small wearing down of confidence and trust over time because I can't believe everything he is telling me.

'I can't stay here,' Ed says, getting up and tipping away his undrunk coffee. 'I'm going to go and pack.'

'You said you'd stay a few days!' I can hear the anxiety in my voice by the way its pitch could smash glass. 'You can keep out of the way of Gwen. Please don't leave now, we're—'

'We're what?' he interrupts. 'We're sorting stuff? I thought so, too, but you just questioned my morals in relation to your *sister*.'

I stand now, not wanting him to have the upper hand.

'So I'm not allowed to question your morals, then? Even though I'm learning to trust you again. I thought questioning would be allowed, seeing as there's no other way I can think of to get the truth out of you.'

He looks as though I've slapped him.

'Not when the questions are in relation to the world's most awful human being. I don't know about other men, but I, for one, wouldn't touch her with a bargepole. You should know that. You shouldn't have to ask me.'

He storms out of the kitchen, leaving me with a red face and a cold coffee. My head drops into my hand and I sigh. It's not supposed to be easy, is it, working things out? More coffee will help. I go to reboil the kettle that Ed always overfills and see Pops smiling at me through the window. I'm mortified that he heard any of that. I wave and the lopsided smile he gives me back tells me he heard it all.

'Here you go,' I say as I hand him a coffee. 'And I made too much food last night so I wondered if you'd like the leftovers? Ed won't need them, he's going home today, and Gwen said I should have gone harder on the salt, so . . .'

I shrug and hand him the Tupperware that I had deliberately made for him and that I'm now doubting. Is this a bit condescending? I don't want Pops to think I'm doing this because I feel sorry for him, it was just so he doesn't have to cook for one for the next few nights. But what if he thinks it's bland and rubbish, too? Do older people's taste buds get less active, just like the rest of them? Maybe I should have added more salt, and some pepper, and . . .

'This smells delightful, Maggie, thank you,' Pops says, his eyes going all misty. 'How kind of you.'

He seals the lid back down and tucks it into his bag. As he straightens up I can hear his bones creaking and popping. Never mind salt and pepper, maybe I should have added cod liver oil and linseed. He rasps out a rattly cough and clears his throat.

'When you reach my age it's almost a kind of rite of passage that we have to pass down our superior knowledge to the young 'uns,' he winks. 'Love is a strange notion. Who we love, how we love. The way it makes us feel alive and hopeful yet scared and newborn all at once. But one thing it must never do is make us question our worth. It can throw difficult questions at us, of course; how would we learn to grow together if it didn't? But the moment that question is "am I good enough for you?" then run for the hills, because love is not an enemy.'

I bite my lip to stop the tears coming as Pops gives my shoulder a squeeze then goes on his way, deadheading the autumnal plants.

Chapter Thirty-Two

Ed's packing when I've calmed down enough to go and look for him. His suitcase is open on the bed, T-shirts and jeans folded neatly on one side, his washbag open on the other. To be honest, I'm not sure he even bothered unpacking it all in the first place.

'Do you really have to go?' I ask him.

He shoves his toothbrush in the bag.

'I think it's for the best,' he says, not meeting my eye. 'Gwen brings out the worst in everyone she's near and I don't want her ruining my chance to make amends with you. It's not for long, then we can be together again back at home and rebuild our life properly.'

He sits on the bed and takes my hand, urging me to sit next to him, so I do.

'Look, I'm sorry I snapped just now,' he says, wrapping an arm over my shoulder. 'I just don't want every argument that we have from now on to boil down to you accusing me of being unfaithful. If we're going to make this work, we need to get past the past.'

He laughs at his own joke. It's not really very funny.

'OK,' I say. 'But that doesn't mean I never get to question your commitment to me, does it? I mean, the whole conversation about trust can't just be taken off the table because it makes you feel guilty.'

I see a faint red wash work its way up Ed's neck. A

sure sign that I've annoyed him, but I think what I've said is fair. If I'm never allowed to talk to Ed about our commitment to each other, or my worries about trust, then I can't hope to be able to reconcile a long-term relationship. But maybe I am being unreasonable. Being back at home seems to have skewed all other reasonable thoughts so far, after all.

'I'd better get back to my bags, I need to get out of here.' He packs the rest of his things in silence, folding each T-shirt with ridiculous precision. When he starts folding the boxers that had been lying on the floor under the bed, I get up and leave.

'Where do you think you're going?' Gwen asks as she catches me turning circles in the hallway because, in actual fact, I have no idea where I'm going or what I'm doing. 'You need to help me in the office.'

Grateful – at least for the direction – I follow Gwen down the stairs and into Mum's office. She clocks the pile of paper on the desk and before I can even think about how grateful I am about already having sorted it, she scoops it all into a black bin liner.

'Gwen,' I say, tentatively, 'don't you think we should check what we're throwing out? What if some of it is to do with the house, or Mum's banking, or something else we now need to deal with because we are in charge?'

'The solicitor who is dealing with the will has all the important documents,' she says, her words clipped. 'He can sort out all of that and just give us our money when he's done. We already know it's half each. I want to get this place on the market as soon as possible.'

I drop my bin bag, my heart hammering.

'Gwen, what about what *I* want?'

'You're in too much of a mess to deal with it all,' she scoffs. 'I'm doing this for us both.'

She carries on filling bin bags with magazines and general detritus from around the office, as though I'm not even there. When she starts on the bookshelf I have to intervene.

'Stop, Gwen, just stop!' I cry. 'Can't you see what you're doing? Throwing everything away won't get rid of the general hatred you feel towards Mum, towards the life she gave us. You need to do something else to vent, because this is *not* OK.'

Gwen stops in the middle of throwing away a copy of *Fifty Shades of Grey* and I almost wish I had stopped her a moment later. The look she is giving me could freeze over even the lustful banter of Mr Grey himself.

'Hatred of Mum? You think I hate *her*?' she spits at me, throwing the book in the bag after all. 'I don't want to rid myself of this house because I want to forget Mum. No, you've got that completely wrong, unsurprisingly. I don't hate Mum, Margaret. Only *you* do.'

The breath catches in my throat as it fills up with claggy cotton wool-like emotions.

'I want to sell the house and be done with everything that we jointly own, so we can start afresh. You've never forgiven Mum, always having a go at her. You're the one who ruined everything and you're just too selfish to see it. Stop blaming Mum on all your failures and start taking some ownership.'

'*What?*' I can barely comprehend what she's saying. Then I'm angry. 'What's my fault, Gwen? That Mum didn't want us around? That she got so drunk most of the time she had no idea where either of us were or what we were doing? Was it my fault that we had to pour ourselves fucking Cheerios for tea because Mum was nowhere to be found? Was it my fault that our school had no idea what was going on at home because we always turned up neatly dressed with our homework done because we had learned to do it ourselves as we were actually pretty good kids? Was it my fault that we were left to fend for ourselves because we had no one else?'

I can't speak anymore and the tears running down my face jumble up the view of Gwen's scowl, but even through them I can tell she's getting ready for her comeback. She is never one to not have the last word.

'She was a good mum until you came along! So yes, all of those things you were just moaning about? They. Are. All. Your. Fault.' With each of those words she pokes me painfully in the shoulder with a jabbing finger. 'I'm getting out of here. It was a mistake to even *think* you'd want to help tidy this place. No wonder Ed can't stand to stay any longer either.'

'Don't you dare!' I hiss at her, wiping my tears away furiously with the back of my hand. 'Don't you dare put all this on me – I was a baby! And don't you dare bring Ed into this conversation. He has nothing to do with Mum.'

'Why is he even here? I saw him the other day looking through some of Mum's things; those financial documents weren't exactly hidden away, were they?' Gwen throws down the bag she has in her hands and storms out of the office, bumping into Ed as she goes.

He's there, looking sheepish, his suitcase in one hand and his phone in the other, bashing out a text. Another flash of jealousy blindsides me, knocking Gwen's accusations completely out of my mind. I want to ask who he's messaging, but this is what he meant, isn't it? I can't just ask him because I'm worried he's messaging another girl. Would I have asked him before all this happened? I can't remember.

'I'm just checking on my taxi to take me to Norwich station. Is everything OK?' he asks, allaying some of my fears.

'Gwen just being Gwen,' I say, hugging him. I don't want him to leave anymore. I need him to stay. 'Be truthful, Ed, are you leaving because of me, or her?'

He strokes my cheek with his thumb and kisses my nose even though it's all snotty and covered in tears.

'Her,' he says, hugging me close. 'And I need to get back to work and earn some bonuses if we're going to buy a house together. It's all going to be OK, Maggie, you'll see. Your mum left us with an answer to our worries, and we can start afresh with never any need to see Gwen again.'

A car pulls up on the gravel outside the door. He hugs me again, his arms not really reaching behind me this time.

'Oh, and Maggie, this arrived for you back at home; it looked important so I thought I'd bring it, forgot about it until I saw it in my case just now.' He hands me an envelope emblazoned with the logo of my work, P&R PR. 'Goodbye, Mags, love you.' And he's off.

'Told you,' Gwen says from the doorway to the kitchen she's just appeared in. 'He was only here to check on your inheritance, not you. You make everyone leave. Except me. You robbed me of any chance I ever had to leave.'

And with that I'm left alone with my thoughts which, trust me, I'd rather not be. In fact, I don't want to be. I march through to the kitchen ready to wage war, the unopened envelope gripped tightly in my sweaty hand.

'Ed loves me! He loved me way before I inherited any money. I don't make everyone leave.' My opening argument is not quite what it should be, because Ed is driving in a taxi to the train station to take him far away from me and my problems.

'I'd bet my half of this house that Ed came to visit you to see what Mum had left you,' Gwen says, and I have a momentary flashback to the papers in his hands as he came charging out of the study. 'He found out, he's leaving again, deal with it. And what about our dad? He was around before you turned up. It's almost as though you made him leave, too. Just give it up, Margaret, deal with it. No. One. Wants. To. Be. Anywhere. Near. You.' She's jabbing at me with her pointy finger again. 'Except that weird old man who hangs around the garden. You're both as lost as each other. You know what they say? Negativity attracts negativity. Weirdness attracts itself.'

The finger poking really hurts, but not as much as the pain of her words. A rapping at the window stops my heart, but it's just Pops. I feel embarrassed at the thought he would have heard what Gwen said about him – and me. I slide the door open.

'Girls,' he says, leaning into the heated kitchen, 'I can hear you out here and I'm half-deaf. Spare a thought for those of us who don't like *EastEnders* or *Jeremy Kyle* and try to sort your problems out amicably.'

Gwen looks apoplectically at Pops. He'd better remove his head from the doorway or she might slice it off with the door that Nick has made so easy to close now. She bites her lips closed; I can tell because she's drawn them right into her mouth and her face looks puce.

'Oh, and Gwen?' he adds, clearly not worried for his own safety. 'There's nothing wrong with weird. It's a lot better than being rude.'

And with that he's off, too, winking at me and holding up his bag where he stored my stew. I want to leap out to the garden and give him a hug. Gwen bashes past me and storms up the stairs muttering about freaks and weirdos as she goes.

'Enjoy your supper!' I yell to Pops and I slide the kitchen door wide open to let in the summer sun.

'Well, this has been a fun day so far,' I say to myself looking at the clock on the wall that looks like it's stopped because there's no way it's only half past eleven.

I take my phone out to send Ed a message telling him I miss him already and wonder if I can ask him about the money – and see Nick's name already there.

We've arrived on the Costa Del Should-have-held-out-for-Italy. Susie delighted in using her limited Spanish to pay for our wine and ended up offering the waiter her hair. She needs to Rosetta some more Stone. Hope you're feeling OK. We'll get searching when I return. Adios hombre. X

I laugh.

Get her to say this next time a waiter brings her some food 'Voy a devorarte'

Well your Spanish certainly outdoes your French! I don't remember you concentrating that much during Mrs Perez' Spanish classes?

I tell Nick that there are a lot of things I learnt that don't involve school then turn my attention to the envelope Ed left me with. Probably a pay slip or something – I have been checking my bank account regularly to make sure P&R haven't totally forgotten about me. What with my unread emails I was at risk of not being able to afford food if they didn't pay me either. I slip the paper out of the shiny white casing and look in disbelief at the written warning glaring back at me with accusatory eyes.

For swearing at your line manager and an inability to meet working commitments. Please regard this as your second written warning (the first from a previous blatant disregard of the office Instagram account).

Urgh. I throw it on the kitchen table and think about how to word my resignation without any swear words.

Faisons cela. Saisissons notre chance. LS

Let's do this. Let's take our chance. LS

Chapter Thirty-Three

A blood-curdling scream pierces the air and makes me momentarily forget my impending unemployment. I instantly know where Gwen is and what has made her scream like a banshee – apart from actually being one, of course. I take the stairs two at a time, rushing around the landing to Mum's room. Just as I suspected, Gwen is there, holding up the remnants of Mum's wedding dress. It's worse than I remember. She's got the only part of the bodice that's still attached to the skirt in her hands, and it's not a big part. On the bed in the background the rest of the bodice is neatly folded. I think back to Nick putting away Mum's dress the day he came over and found me a snivelling mess. He could have just thrown the dress into her room as he was leaving, but he must have taken the time to make it look neat, even though I'd ripped it to shreds.

'What have you done?' She's not shouting now, her face is drained. It's actually scarier than shouty Gwen, like she's finally about to lose the plot.

Her eyes look like they're getting misty. I don't think I've ever seen Gwen cry before. Not properly. Not except the tears for attention like the ones she produced at Mum's funeral. These look like they might be from the depths of her icy-white heart. And they're making me feel guilty.

'Look, Gwen, I can explain,' I say. 'You know I found Mum's wedding dress on my first night back here? It made me feel, well, it reminded me that Mum never cared about how I felt.'

'Why does *everything* have to be about *you*?' she asks me.

I walk into the room, feeling a great sense of heaviness weighing down my legs. I perch on the bed next to the dress and burrow a hand in the lace part.

'This has never been about me,' I say, shaking my head. 'I asked Mum a few months before she died if I could borrow her dress for when Ed and I get married and she told me she didn't know where it was. Then I saw it, pride of place in her dressing room, at her funeral.'

'And how is that not completely all about you? Maybe she knew you and Ed would never get married,' Gwen says, the venom back in her voice. She drops the remnants of the dress onto the bed next to me and sits down on the floor, propped up by the wall. Gwen never sits on the floor, that shows how much she doesn't want to sit with me on the bed. 'Anyone in their right mind can see you and Ed will never get married.'

'What's that supposed to mean?' I know I shouldn't ask; I don't need to hear how Gwen thinks my relationship is as doomed as the rest of my whole life, but like a scab, I can't help but pick it.

'Ed doesn't want to be with you,' she says, shifting her bum on the thick carpet. 'He wants all *this*. He doesn't want *you*, he wants what you have. And it's obvious you don't really want to be with him either.'

I open my mouth to retaliate. And at one point I would have done. But now I'm not sure what to say. Getting back together with Ed had been my priority and had thrown me so asunder that I couldn't think straight. But now Gwen has put these ideas in my head I can't help but think of the conversations Ed and I have been having over the last few days. The '*let's buy somewhere and pay off our debt*', the '*your mum has enough in her savings to pay off our cards, let alone what the house is worth*'. The excitement Ed tried to hide when I talked about selling, and the disappointment he could barely conceal when I said I wanted to stay. Gwen is right. Plus, my feelings for Nick, whatever they transpire to be, have shown me that maybe I don't want to be with Ed – I just don't want him to be the one to leave.

'What makes it so obvious?' I ask Gwen.

'When Alex and I are together we don't have to try to *be* around each other. We can just get on with our own lives. You and Ed, you're tugging each other in directions you don't want to go in. You always have been. You were so insular when you got together that you moulded into one person with a split personality. You can't just let each other *be* like Alex and I because you're so used to doing everything together.'

'Not everything,' I say, surprised at how much Gwen was paying attention to my relationship. 'The reason I came back wasn't to look through Mum's things now she's dead, it was because Ed was sleeping with someone else and I had nowhere else to go. He came here to sort things out between us, but they've been just as difficult as before. Maybe you're right about the money. Oh, and my job told me to take some time out and while I've been away they've decided to reprimand me enough for me to never want to go back.'

'Well . . .' Gwen shrugs.

It's the first time we've sat down and talked without raising our voices at each other in so long that I can't even remember when it last happened.

'I only tried on Mum's dress because I wanted to see what it looked like.'

'That's not the entire truth, is it?'

I really wish Gwen would stop reading my mind and telling me all my inner secrets.

'No, I guess not,' I say, chewing my cheek. 'I think I wanted to say a big "screw you" to the woman who hated me so much. To get in the dress she lied to me about.'

'And how did that make you feel?'

'Stupid,' I say, realising it's the first time I've said it out loud. 'That there was no way trying on Mum's dress would make up for years of her neglect, just because she didn't want me to have it. But it looked good on me, and that made me feel slightly less stupid. *That* was a bonus. But then I remembered that I probably will never get married, especially after Ed's, you know, indiscretion. And then you made me feel even worse when you called. So, I tried to get out of the dress in a rush and that's when it ripped.'

Gwen looks at the tatters next to me on the bed.

'You did *that* getting out of it?' If I'm not mistaken there could be the glimmer of a smile forming on Gwen's lips.

'Not exactly.' I'm not sure if I should just play innocent, say I hacked the dress with a pair of scissors because I hated the way it made me feel. Gwen has already told me what she thinks of my search for our dad, but maybe if I can show her how much they loved each other Gwen might feel differently. A split-second decision that could go either way.

'I . . . I found something in the dress,' I say, too late to go back now. 'Wait here.'

My room feels quiet without the ebb and flow of another body in it and I enjoy the peace for a moment, rummaging in my dungarees for the letters. But now I have them in my hand I'm reluctant to share them with Gwen. It felt right to discover them with Nick, to try and read them to Ed. They had, in their own ways, been positive about my discovery. But Gwen has always found a way to belittle me and I don't think this is going to go any differently. I flick through them quickly from beginning to end, looking at the love story that I know developed from Nick's translations, from love's first flicker to marriage. Tucking them in my pocket I quickly make my bed, cursing Ed for not doing it as I pull the duvet up under my pillows and fold the blanket over the foot of the bed where I will just throw it off later tonight.

My hands feel sweaty as I make my way back down the corridor to Mum's room.

Tell her.

Don't tell her.

Tell her.

Don't tell her.

My footsteps tap out the words, a rubbish game of he loves me, he loves me not. Gwen has moved, just onto the bed so I hover around the doorway.

'Well?' She's got a sour face back on as her fingers weave through the ripped lace.

Handing over the letters, my eyes study her face as she reads them with the knowledge of French I know she has. Her own pinched face recoils as she realises what she's reading. She shakes her head so much her ponytail swishes.

'What is this?' She looks disgusted. 'What am I reading?'

'EB and LS?' I say, as though it's an answer. And it should be an answer, but her face still looks confused. 'LS must be Dad's initials. These are why I have been looking for Dad. Where Nick's got his leads from. I thought I'd found him on an ancestry website I joined, but it can't have been him because he would have been ancient, and now my free trial is up and I can't afford it anymore.' My voice quietens to a hush.

She keeps shaking her head. 'So?'

'So,' I say, lifting the dress from beside her and shaking it, 'these are what made me cut up Mum's wedding dress. They were sewn into the lining of the bodice.'

'Why on earth . . .?' Gwen starts, looking back at the letters.

'Because she was in love. Because she once was someone with a heart,' I answer. 'Nick and I started looking for Dad because I wanted to have a family I could talk to.'

'And you thought that our deadbeat dad could give you that even though you've never met him, yet I've been in your life for your whole thirty-two bloody years and you've never asked me to talk to you?'

'Because you talk to me like *this*! I thought a dad might at least let me talk without making me feel two foot tall. That maybe he left because Mum was too difficult to handle, not because of me. I guess I wanted to ask him all the questions that I've been storing up for my whole life.'

Gwen is still shaking her head and I can't believe she's not going to let me get away with this.

'You just don't get it, do you?'

'No, Gwen.' I can feel my blood starting to heat my cheeks. 'We thought we found someone and Nick's been trying to find their wedding certificate. We thought it was a guy called Leonard, but it wasn't him in the end as he's still married. But the feeling I had when I thought we'd found him felt right. I don't have any regrets. Oh, Gwen, look at how romantic he once was! How he loved our mum with all his being. Don't tell me that's not worth fighting to find?'

She can't argue with that, it's written in black and white right in front of her, in a script that looks just like mine. But she does.

'You're deluded.' She jumps down from the bed and waves the letters in my face. 'Mum didn't sew these into her wedding dress because they're a show of affection between her and Dad!'

'What? Gwen, are you just arguing with me for argument's sake now?' I shout. 'Because I thought we were having a grown-up conversation. Give those back to me before you rip them.'

'Like Mum's dress?' She shoves them into my hands, crumpling the old paper. 'Dad isn't some sort of romantic hero, rescuing Mum from a sad childhood and dead parents with a cape and a Shakespearean tongue.'

'You don't know that!' I yell, throwing my arms up in disbelief at her arrogance.

'Yes, Margaret, I do,' she says, and the room drops to a deathly silence. 'Mum never *got* married. Our dad never asked her. God knows why Mum had that dress in the first place, but Dad had nothing to do with it, or those wretched letters. His name doesn't even begin with an L. Our *dad* is called Dave and he lives in a semi-detached house in a suburb south of Norwich.'

My jaw drops and my heart goes with it.

Chapter Thirty-Four

Then . . .

We're all in a circle on the living room floor, trying not to think about the damp patches. I'm sitting next to Perdita, Brian the football captain on the other side. His hand keeps sneaking over towards me and grazing my thigh, but I can't move any closer to Perdie or I'll be sitting on her lap. Finn, a boy in the year above, is opposite Perdita and they're giving each other the goo-goo eyes. I crane my head to check where Nick is. There's no way I'm playing spin the bottle unless he's joining in, too. Not if Brian and James and a square-nosed guy from my maths class, whose name I don't know, are playing. The whole point of spin is that I get to kiss who I want, isn't it? And Nick and I have been catching each other's eye all night, from the moment he handed me a bottle of blue WKD.

Perdita grabs the empty tequila bottle and spins it, tapping the bottom so it lands on Finn. She jumps over the bottle and dives on top of him to whooping cheers from the rest of the group. Panic is rising in my chest as Nick is nowhere to be seen. Maybe spin the bottle is too childish for him. What was I thinking? Of course spin the bottle is too childish for him! I start to scramble to my feet when Brian grabs my wrist and pulls me back down.

'No, you don't,' he says, his beery breath making me want to gag. 'You haven't had a go yet. Club rules. You sit down, you spin.'

I have no idea what stupid club he is a part of, but I am definitely not a member. I try to shake my hand free, but Brian's grip is too strong. He pulls a bit harder and I sit down again with a bump. The crowds behind me move in a bit. I can feel a bead of sweat trickling down underneath my shiny tight top, while others start tickling my hair. Brian still has a hold of my wrist as James takes his turn to spin. He looks at me and gives me a huge smile and the WKD starts churning in my stomach. I look around for help. Perdita is still snogging the face off Finn and everyone else is now too engrossed in who the bottle is about to land on to care that I'm being held captive by the captain of the football team.

Am I being too dramatic? I mean, Brian is the captain of the football team, loads of girls would love to be sitting next to him as he protests that they stay. Nick is still nowhere to be seen. He'd understand. But even if he is still in the room, the way people are standing over us, watching, no one except Brian and me can tell he has a hold of my hand so tightly it's making my fingers tingle.

The bottle slows to a stop on me and I feel a violent urge to get out of here. My WKD is sitting in my throat again now, my heart rate through the roof. People are clapping and cheering and James gets up off the floor and launches himself at me. Halfway there, still in mid-air, Nick appears from over James' shoulder.

'Not this one, mate,' he says and a girl who I know from swimming offers herself up to James on my behalf.

Chapter Thirty-Five

I can't hear what Gwen is saying over the thumping of blood in my ears. I can't have heard her right. She said our dad is called Dave and lives a normal life only a few miles away from where we grew up. That can't be right, for so many reasons. Huge reasons like: why didn't he come and see us if he lives so close? Why sign off his letters with an LS? How did I not know Mum never married? How the hell does Gwen know all this and what the actual fuck does it mean that she did?

I fall down onto the bed, just about making it before my legs give way. I had no idea that jelly legs were so real until right this very moment. I flump; my body has gained ten stone in the last few seconds and forgotten how to breathe.

'What?' I manage to get the word out before my bottom lip starts to wobble.

'Yeah,' Gwen says, waving her hand in the air as if to dismiss what she said like it isn't the biggest bombshell she's ever dropped. Like she hasn't just changed my whole life with the sentence she just said. 'This is probably why Mum kept him a secret from you. Look at you, jumping to find him at the first opportunity, not caring why he left in the first place, not caring why he stayed away when he could dash over here in his Fiesta and give us both a hug and some pocket money and still be the world's best dad in your eyes.'

She laughs. She actually laughs. She's breaking my heart so much more thoroughly than normal and finding it funny.

'You know what car he drives?'

'Oh God, Margaret, do me a favour and grow up. So what if I know what car he drives?'

I can't stand it anymore. I shoot up off the bed, not caring if I collapse under the weight of what Gwen is saying. My hands fly through my hair and I want to tug at it, to tear it out and feel real, physical pain and not this razor-sharp stabbing at my heart. Tears are falling down my cheeks, I know. I can feel their heat as they drop from my chin and hit the thick, luxurious carpet that Mum had fitted in her bedroom only. It's all coming flooding towards me. The hatred that everyone in the house felt towards me growing up, the reason I left as soon as I could. They were laughing at me behind my back all this time. *Poor Maggie wants to find her dad.*

'So what?' I yell in Gwen's face. 'So what? Gwen, we are talking about our dad, a dad I never knew existed, let alone if he even had a car. Can't you see how wrong this is? Even you, with your cold useless heart, must be able to see how evil keeping something like this from me is?'

Something in Gwen shifts and her face turns a deep shade of scarlet. She stands up from the bed and is so close to my face I can smell her perfect shampoo and her subtly expensive perfume.

'If my heart is so cold and useless, how come Mum told me about Dad? How come my husband isn't sleeping with someone else? How come I have my shit sorted? Do you ever look at me and not feel jealous enough to be unkind?'

Her question throws me, but for once I cannot let her gaslight me over this. I need to summon up the courage to tell her exactly how I have felt over the last few years.

Her face is still so close to mine it's hard not to see Mum in her . . . and myself.

'You've been lying to me about my dad,' I say, backing away now. I feel the warm wallpaper behind my shaking, sweaty hands. 'You'll be lucky if I ever talk to you again, never mind being unkind to you.'

'Why the hell would I tell you the truth about Dad?' she hisses at me. 'So you can scare him off again? So you can blunder into his life with your usual grace? Little old Dave Appleby didn't want to know you the first time around, Margaret, so he's certainly not going to want to know you now.'

'Get out!' I scream. 'Get out. Get out. Get out!'

I flap my arms at Gwen and a part of me wants to flap them so hard I knock her to the ground where she has been pushing me to ever since I was born. But I can't bring myself to do it, I know I'm better than that. She looks scared, though, as she scrambles down under my arms and around to the relative safety of the landing. But it's not enough.

'I don't want you here, Gwen. Not at all. GET OUT!'

Her eyes are wide now, her perfect blue irises tiny amongst the whites that have grown exponentially since I started standing up for myself.

'B-but it's my house, too,' she stammers, tripping a little over her own feet as she tries and fails to walk away quicker.

'Oh, *now* you claim it belongs to both of us?' I can't stop. I'm walking towards her as she's stepping backwards. I can see the stairs looming behind her. She's not even thinking about the stairs; I can tell she just wants to get as far away from me as possible. Her heel is right at the edge and I see her lift her other leg. 'Stop!'

I grab her arm and pull her towards me. For a split

second I think she is going to wallop me one, but she notices the stairs and looks at my hand gripped around her forearm and her eyes fill with tears.

'Let me go,' she says, her voice wobbling.

So I do. My hand relaxes and my own tears carry on as I watch Gwen descend the stairs, listen to her grabbing her handbag and phoning her perfect husband. I sink to the carpet and lean against the bannisters, their pointy edges poking my back and making me at least feel something. And I stay there as Gwen leaves the house, slamming the door so hard the pictures in the hallway downstairs rattle loudly in protest. Then I'm on my own again.

'Dish out the food, I'll get the blankets,' Perdita is shouting back down the stairs to Phillip as she takes them two at a time towards me.

The sun has set behind the house now and I'm sitting in the dark in the same position Gwen left me in. I have no idea how much time has passed, only that it has, and I still feel like I'm losing my marbles.

Perdita takes me gently around the chest and pulls me up to standing. My legs creak and groan at the movement, pins and needles flooding through my knees and feet. I welcome the pain.

'Jeez, Mags,' Perdita says, lifting one of my arms around her shoulder and giving me a kiss on the cheek. 'What on earth happened to you?'

'Gwen.' I don't want to tell her about my dad yet. 'How did you know?'

'I had no idea, love,' she says, and we take each step together like a three-legged obstacle race. 'We arranged to have dinner at yours tonight, remember?'

'Nope.'

'Sure you do,' she says, plopping me on my sofa and covering me in a fluffy blanket she must have found somewhere. With a plate of curry on a tray on my lap all I need is a pair of fluffy slippers and I'm ready to collect my pension and start watching *Diagnosis Murder*. I relay this to Perdita and Phillip who snuggle up next to me with their own food.

'Are you saying you don't watch that already?' Phillip asks, throwing forkfuls of madras into his mouth. 'I love daytime TV, though I always get suckered into donating money to animal charities when I see their sob stories during ITV3 runs of Agatha Christie. Especially the donkeys with their overgrown wonky hooves that make them look like elves. Or those poor bears wrapped in chains and looking like hipster men whose beards are out of control. I'm always getting into trouble with adding standing orders from the joint account to help the poor sods. I can't help it, they're all so adorable.'

'Yes, yes, we get it, you're an angel, Phillip,' Perdita interrupts, dunking a peshwari naan into a vindaloo. 'But right now there are more important things to worry about than wonky donkeys, no matter how cute they are.'

She turns to look at me as I push bits of lamb around a pool of korma.

'What did Gwen do? And where's Ed?' she asks me, taking a great bite of her curry-covered naan.

'Oh, you know,' I say breezily. 'She was just Gwen being Gwen. Ed left because Gwen was being Gwen. Plus, he was only after Mum's inheritance, so I think we're actually over now. I just need to tell him.'

I shove a mouthful of food in so I don't have to say anything else. Perdita rubs my foot through the blanket, leaving a blood-red greasy mark on the material.

'Are you sure you don't want to talk about it more?'

I shake my head.

'OK, love. Phillip, get that TV on and find some trash that doesn't include mutilated animals that will make us all cry.'

Phillip hits the remote with his elbow, his own hands too greasy. The TV blares and we settle down to watch a night of *X-Files*. Sexy Mulder is enough to keep my mind off most things normally but tonight thoughts of Gwen's betrayal and the abandonment by both my mum and dad can't be drowned out by a smouldering gaze or an undone top button. But I love my best friends for trying. We eat in a silence that doesn't feel the need to be filled with inane chatter or digging questions about my being found curled up in the foetal position at the top of the stairs. Phillip occasionally gets off his seat to refill my glass of really fancy red wine, but other than that we're at peace with each other. Food done, Perdita wraps her arm around my shoulder and I lean against her, my eyes feeling heavy. As I start to nod off, I can't help my brain kick-starting again, the annoying way it does just as I feel myself let go.

'How did you really know I needed you?' I ask them.

'Ed,' Phillip says as Perdita thumps him hard on the shoulder. 'Apparently Gwen messaged Ed to tell him you'd finally gone crazy. He messaged me to see if it was true.'

'Right,' I say, closing my eyes and letting sleep embrace me, but not before wondering how I'm going to break it to Ed that I don't love him anymore.

Pour toujours, je ferme ma main autour de la tienne et je sais que c'est là qu'elle appartient.

Forever, I close my hand around yours and I know that's where it belongs.

Chapter Thirty-Six

So we're back in the UK. Susie is never speaking Spanish ever again. What did you tell her to say? I've been doing some more digging on the plane, can we meet up? Nick.

It takes my brain a while to figure out who I am and what I'm doing sleeping on the sofa under a blanket that smells like sweat. I lift my armpit and have a little sniff; it's not me. As my eyes start to focus on my own living room I remember Phillip, Perdita, dinner and Mulder. Despite the sinking pit of despair that is now my stomach, I manage a smile at the memory.

There's a note scrawled on the back of an empty naan bag in Perdita's doctor-hand. As I'm trying to decipher it I curse her silently for not letting Phillip write that they'd had to go home as Phillip had dad duties and Perdita had a nose-job first thing then had to pack to head back to London. Surely it can't be nearly October already? I need to check, because I think after two written warnings P&R can kick me out for any misdemeanours, no matter how small. I check the date on my phone and reread Nick's message so I can reply.

Welcome back trepid explorer of weekend away in the Costa Del Horriblis. Sorry, I wasn't expecting Susie to actually say it . . . I have one last huge favour to ask of you. Are you free this morning?

Nick replies in a smile-inducing quick amount of time.

Right. I'd pass your apologies on but Susie is taking some time out from me (what does that even mean?). Our trip (that she organised) wasn't quite up to her normal standards. Anyway, I'll stop using so many brackets now and get up and dressed and be over as soon as I can.

Nick is typing to me in bed with no clothes on? I'd type back that I'm still fully clothed from yesterday and sleeping on the sofa but my battery is nearly dead and explaining that in person is probably much easier. I get up and drag my body to the shower.

'Whoa,' Nick exclaims as we're motoring down the dual carriageway towards the suburbs on the south side of Norwich. 'So Gwen not only knew all about your dad, she has known about him her whole life? She even knows what kind of car he drives and where he lives? That's . . . I don't know what it is, except hurtful and totally Gwen – and no wonder you're not talking to her anymore.'

'She didn't actually know what kind of car he drives or where he lives, I think she was just making a really stupid point. I searched for him on the registry this morning to find his address. Good old Google.'

I stare out at the churned fields flying past us as they change into pockets of new build houses rammed so close to the road that their back gardens may as well have a Little Chef in a shed to earn a second income. Nick has a post-holiday glow that I want to talk to him about but I don't want to ask about Susie in case it's still a bit raw, and how can I ask him about a holiday without talking about who he went with? Anyway, he's been too engrossed in the revelations about my dad. Butterflies are having a

214

rave in my empty stomach with last night's leftover wine. I should have eaten, but the thought made me feel sick.

'And his name doesn't even begin with an L, or have initials anything like LS?' Nick asks, checking his rear-view mirror and overtaking an Asda lorry. 'That's so weird. Maybe it was a nickname or a cute lover's name? Luscious Scrotum or something like that?'

I burst out laughing and whack Nick on the shoulder, grateful to him for being able to make me forget, just for a millisecond, that I'm about to meet my dad for the first time ever in my life.

'Lickable Shins?'

'Ew, enough, enough,' I cry through tears of laughter. 'Stop before you make me visualise anything else to do with a man I'm about to come face to face with! I do not want the taste of his shins to be the first thing my brain thinks of, thank you very much.'

'Long Schlong?' he adds, pulling off the dual carriageway and turning left at the roundabout below.

I howl with laughter and my sides ache with the pain of it. So much so that I don't notice Nick turning into a small road with identikit detached houses with neat front gardens and brick driveways until he's parked up outside one with a Ford Fiesta nestled by the garage. Maybe Gwen did know, after all.

My heart is hammering in my mouth as I take in the white net curtains and the tubs of geraniums either side of the door. It looks like a family home.

'Do you want me to come with you?' Nick asks, taking my cold sweaty hand in his.

I shake my head.

'I think this is something I need to do on my own, but I appreciate you asking, thank you,' I say. My voice sounds weird.

'I'll wait here, then,' he says. 'For as long as you need me to.'

I nod, my eyes fixed on the house, my breathing ragged.

'I think you need to get out now, though,' Nick adds.

'Maybe I should just email him first?'

'Maggie!'

'OK, OK, I'm going.'

If my heart hammers any harder I'm at risk of having a coronary. Maybe Dad is a doctor, that would be handy at a time like this. The car door feels heavy but I push it open and turn to Nick.

'Good luck,' he says, his eyes smiling, and I shut the door and walk towards the house.

I need luck. I don't even know what I'm going to say. How do you start a conversation like the one I'm about to have? It's too late to think about it now, though, as I watch my finger press the doorbell and hear the shrill ringing pierce the quiet street. There's someone in, I can hear them behind the door, rustling something and the click of a lock. It opens and I'm greeted by a boy. A young man, really. He can't be much older than mid-twenties. He cocks his head and waits for me to speak. He's assured and calm. I most definitely am not any of the above.

'Um,' I say, thinking this might be my half-brother and willing myself not to blurt that out. 'I'm looking for Dave?'

The young man gives me a cheeky smile and leans back into the house.

'Dad, it's someone for you!' he shouts. 'I'm off, I'll see you when I'm finished.'

He walks past me and gets into the Fiesta, reversing it confidently down the drive and narrowly missing Nick's old Volvo. I don't know what I'd been expecting. For Dave to have been sitting around waiting for me to get in contact so he could start a family life? Of course he has another family. I want to run after the Fiesta and leave now, too.

What am I doing here?

I turn back to the house and he's already there, standing in the doorway, wearing a grubby vest, waiting for me to speak, to tell him who I am and why I'm knocking on his door at eleven on a weekday morning.

'H-hi,' I stutter.

'Hello,' he says, with just a teeny lilt of a Norfolk accent. 'I'm not looking to buy anything, and I already give to Oxfam with regular donations from the kids and wife, and I'm a devoted atheist who is probably going to hell anyway so I'm a lost cause on pretty much every count.'

He laughs the laugh of a man who spends his time in a bookies when they still allowed smoking. I study his face, frantically trying to see in him whatever it was that Mum did. Maybe it's not him.

'Dave?'

His expression gets curious now.

'I'm sorry, who are you?'

'My name is Margaret Burnett.'

The colour drains from his face. He steps towards me and for a split second I think he's going to reach out and take me in his arms. My heart soars. But he sidesteps past me and pulls the door shut behind him.

'What are you doing here?' he whispers.

I feel sick.

'Mum died last month and I found something of yours. I was just bringing it back for you,' I stutter, taking the pages from my pocket and handing them to Dave even though I don't want to but it was the only thing I could think of in the moment. 'And I wanted to finally meet you.'

217

He takes the notes from me, his expression growing even more confused. His hands flick through them, his eyes darting over the words. He hands them back to me.

'These aren't mine. I can't speak foreign.'

'B-but . . .' I stammer. I think about the wedding dress and what Gwen said about Mum never marrying. And now I feel stupid. 'Are – are you even my dad?'

He hushes me and takes my arm to lead me back to the bottom of the driveway. I catch Nick's eye from the car and shake my head as he reaches for the door handle.

'I said to Lizzie when this all happened the first time around that I didn't want to have a family with her.'

I baulk at the brutality of his words and the familiarity by which he refers to my mum.

'Sorry if that seems harsh, but it was the truth at the time and still is now. I have a family already. And I did then, too. But Lizzie was determined to have Gwen. And we couldn't really keep away from each other – you know how it is – so when she got pregnant again I decided that enough was enough and cut all contact. She was talking about marriage and the like but I was already engaged to someone else. I couldn't very well up and leave one family for another.'

I have no idea how I am holding it together, only that I cannot believe the utter tripe coming out of this man's mouth.

'Look,' he adds, kind of squeezing at my shoulder, 'I'm sure you're a lovely person and everything, but I just don't want this all coming out now. And getting to know you and your sister would mean that happening. We've managed this far without each other, haven't we?'

'I . . .' I have no idea how to answer that.

'I am sorry about your mum, I was sad to learn she had died. She was a wonderful, if pretty bossy, woman.'

He turns to walk back to the house but halfway up the path he looks back and adds, 'Can you tell your sister what I said about this? It's just she likes to come and stare at the house sometimes and it's a bit weird, you know? Good luck with everything.'

Good luck with everything?

'Do you know what I think is weird, Dave?' I say, my voice raised so he can hear me from near the house. 'A dad who doesn't want to get to know his own children.'

I fling open the gate and storm away to the car, my heart ready to burst out of my chest.

'Drive!' I say to Nick as he starts to ask me what happened.

Because if I have to think about what just happened now, and actually how alone I really am, I don't think my heart will cope.

Si l'amour était facile, tout le monde le prendrait pour acquis.

If love was easy, everyone would take it for granted.

Chapter Thirty-Seven

We drive the long way home, Ocean Colour Scene crooning gently in the background. Neither Nick nor I say anything. I can't, and I think Nick can tell by the tears once again streaming down my cheeks that now is not the best time to ask how the father-daughter reunion went.

What did Mum see in a selfish idiot like Dave?

The question is going around and around in my mind. Yes, Mum may have been selfish in her own way, but she was beautiful and worldly and clever and friendly. Dave looked like he was a wife-beater vest away from a Stella advert. Even his house had been vanilla-coated wannabe bourgeois. He is worlds away from the woman I knew to be my mum.

Nick drives slowly as he takes the exit from the bypass and starts on the winding roads back to my home. It dawns on me, and I don't know when it happened, but at some point over the last few weeks I have started calling the house my home. And it is. It may be full of memories that I'd rather not have, but there are good ones there, too. Tucked in amongst the neglect and Mum's lavish parties, there are the hugs and the hair brushing and the games that Gwen and I played before it all went wrong. Maybe this is my chance to put the bad memories to rest and learn to love the house.

'I was thinking about moving back to Norfolk. Now I don't know. What should I do?' I ask Nick as he opens his window to the sun now filling the sky.

'That's a loaded question, Maggie,' he says, his eyes on the road. 'You need to ask yourself what's important to you. I can't make that choice for you.'

'No,' I say, 'but you can tell me what you think.'

He rubs his face with his hand. His hair is all over the place, the curls sticking up towards the roof of the car.

'I think what you need is a bit of TLC – and I know just the person.'

He pulls the car onto the driveway of his parents' house and I realise he must have been bringing me here all along. He's out of the car and opening my door before I can protest, not that I think I want to. I ruffle my hands through my hair and try desperately to wipe the tearstains from my cheeks.

'Stop it,' he says, taking my arm. 'You look lovely, as always.'

My cheeks heat, which is a positive as this should dry off any leftover tears.

His mum gives me a huge hug as Nick ambles into the kitchen and straight over to the table where she had been sitting doing the crossword with a cuppa and some digestives which he promptly dunks then eats whole.

'Hello, love,' she says, not asking how I am, which I'm very grateful for. 'Here, take a seat and I'll get some more tea in the pot.'

I sit down at their kitchen table, a large, marked and stained wooden farmhouse table with a vase of flowers in the middle and a few cats lying underneath in the patches of sun that stream through from the conservatory attached. The kitchen itself smells like flowers and roast lamb and my stomach lets out a cry for help. Mrs Forster tops up the plate of biscuits and tells me to help myself as she puts a steaming mug of tea in front of me. There's sugar in a little bowl on the table and a jug of milk. I help myself and add a sugar even though I don't normally.

'Thank you, Mrs Forster,' I say when I've finished a digestive.

'Oh, please,' she says, coming to sit with me at the table. Nick is lying on the floor playing with the cats. 'Call me Ivy, love.'

She sips her own tea.

'Nick told me what the pair of you have been doing,' she says, her voice kind. 'Is that where you've been today? Looking for your dad?'

I nod. I can feel pressure building in my throat again and fear the tears that are inevitable if I open my mouth to do anything other than eat more biscuits.

'Can I tell you something, love?' Ivy asks me. 'About your mum?'

I keep nodding.

'You know at the party you spoke to me about your mum, when I told you how much alike you were? Well, we grew up together, your mum and I. Same year at school. We were close, not best friends, but we spent a lot of time together. Then, as we got older and we left school and started our own families, Elizabeth and I fell out of touch. I had met Nick's dad and we spent a lot of our early days travelling around the world in an old camper van, something your mum used to say she would love to do. But I guess when your grandma got poorly, she had to stay at home to help your grandad with everything.

'When we eventually came home to Norfolk your mum was pregnant with Gwen. She was very cagey about the

222

father but said it was a man she loved with all her heart and that was what mattered. She'd gone from this outgoing, wonderful girl who had the time for anyone who needed it, to a woman who looked so fragile that a strong wind would knock her over. I was worried. All her friends were, but she hushed us up and grew more and more contained. I blame myself, sometimes, for not pushing harder to get through to her, especially when she lost her parents so close to each other.' Ivy looks out into the conservatory as she finishes her tea. 'Still, she bloomed when Gwen was born, which was wonderful to see, and Gwen was such a happy baby. There was more talk of the father – in fact, your mum started talking about a wedding; I think she even got herself a dress. She was happy and the light in her seemed to return.

'She always loved you, Maggie. But I think everything went awry for a while when she fell pregnant with you. She was over the moon to be having another baby. I remember her saying that she'd need to get the wedding dress altered. But the next time I pressed her on it she said it was over and that she was on her own. Gwen became more difficult, I think – she was at that age – and I was pregnant with Nick at the time and seeing one of your friends falling apart is so hard.

'We saw each other a few times when our babies were born, introduced you two when you were only a few months old.'

Nick's head clunks the underside of the table as he makes an exclamation.

'But she was never the same. Family didn't seem important to her anymore; she was more interested in parties and drinking. So, we fell out of the same circle. I don't blame your mum; I blame the man who caused her so much hurt.

'Which I why is wanted to speak to you about your dad.'

Nick's head makes another loud bang as he scurries out from under the table and a cat flees in disgust.

'Mum,' he starts but Ivy holds up her hand to stop him.

'Let me say this, Nick,' she says. 'Maggie, I think maybe he's best left unfound.'

My bottom lip starts wobbling.

'It's a bit late for that,' I say.

I thought my body would be all out of tears from the last few days, but I was wrong. I shake so violently I spill the cold tea from my mug. Nick takes it very gently from my hands and puts it on the table. His hand rests on my shoulder and I feel ashamed as I tell them what Dave had said to me as he'd sent me on my way, rejected. No longer can I hope that there will be a member of my own family who doesn't despise me. No, I am truly on my own.

'What an utter shite!' Ivy says, after I've finished what I can and the words are starting to sound like a jumbled mess. 'Give her a hug, Nick, don't just stand there like a lemon. Maggie, we're all here for you, you don't deserve that. And *he* absolutely does not deserve to have a daughter like you.'

Nick half-bends, half-squats to hug me. He whispers sorry in my ear and his hair tickles my face. It should feel all sorts of awkward, given the angle and the kind-hearted demands from his mum, but it doesn't. It feels like the most natural thing in the world. Even when the hug goes on for longer than it politely should.

Ivy gets up and starts pottering around the kitchen. A waft of lamb refills the room as she opens the oven to check on it.

'You'll stay for supper,' she says, not asking again in that way that makes me feel like I've missed out on so much unconditional love.

Nick lets go of me, his knees cracking as he takes the seat his mum has just left. Our eyes are drawn to each other and I can feel a familiar pull in my chest as my heart races.

'I'd better not, thank you, Ivy,' I say, not looking away from Nick. 'I need to get home. I need to talk to Gwen. And I need to decide what I'm going to do about my job in London that's hanging by a thread.'

Ivy drops the pan she'd been holding with a clatter in the sink and mutters a whispered swear.

'Oh, you're not going back to London, are you?' she asks.

I nod. 'I guess eventually I've got to,' I say.

'What?' Nick says, standing suddenly from his chair. 'But I thought . . . Let me at least drive you home.'

'No, honestly, it's OK, thank you, I've a taxi coming in a few minutes,' I say, grateful for the local taxi app that can order a lift at the surreptitious click of a button. 'And thank you, Ivy, for being honest with me about Mum. And for the tea and biscuits that I seem to have decimated, sorry!'

'There's more where they came from. Anytime you want to talk about her, I'm here, love.' She takes my face in her hands and kisses my forehead. I'm overwhelmed with love for this woman I barely know, because it's been forever since someone touched me touch that hasn't been a precursor to some kind of sexual encounter. In fact, I've never really known the love of a familial hug.

'Come on, then,' Nick says, and we leave the warm, comforting kitchen that smells like Sunday roast. 'I'll walk you out.'

We head out to the pavement to wait for the car. Nick stops at the roadside, poking the fallen leaves in the gutter with the toe of his shoe. His conker-coloured eyes find mine and my hands shake a little as I walk closer to him. The air around me is thinner than normal, I'm sure. He tilts his head as if to ask me a question, but I'm not sure of the answer.

'Thank you,' I whisper.

Nick scrunches up his nose. 'For walking you out? Any time, Maggie.'

'For now. For earlier. For the whole time I've been back in Norfolk.'

He leans into me, his eyes still searching, his breath catching in his throat. My own lungs constrict as I'm pulled towards him with a force I can't control. Our lips are only inches apart when a car drives around the corner and he flinches and pulls back as though hit by static electricity. Which, to be fair, could have been more than possible.

'Sorry,' he grunts, shoving his hands in his pocket. 'We shouldn't be doing this. It's not what I do. It's been great having you back home, Maggie. But I guess this is it now! You can head back to London, back to Ed.'

What's not what he does? A relationship? Me? I have no idea what has just happened between us. I climb into the taxi, my face burning enough to hot-wire it.

'Goodbye, Nick,' I say through the open window as the car pulls away from the curb.

'Goodbye, Maggie,' he replies, air escaping his body. And I miss the rest of what he says as the car speeds off down the road.

When we pull into my driveway, the taxi driver starts to say something, but I can't hear what it is over the sound of my own shouts for the car to stop. I'm opening the car door and jumping out before he's had a chance to pull to a complete standstill.

Pops is lying there on the gravel. Face down. Not moving.

Chapter Thirty-Eight

Then . . .

Nick grabs my hand and pulls me closer to standing. Brian must be either so hammered or so shocked that his grip loosens enough for my hand to slip through his.

This is it, I think, as Nick draws me across the circle of people and holds me close, his body warm through my squeaky pleather dress.

The whoops and cheers of the rest of Year Eleven are echoing now, as though they're watching from down a tunnel. Or maybe Nick and I are the ones in the tunnel. Whoever it is in a tunnel, there's no getting away from the fact that Nick is about to kiss me in front of the many partygoers congregating in the living room. Which, by the feel of the encroaching crowd, is growing exponentially by the second, geed on probably by the increasing volume of cheering.

I've never been so excited and so high as I am now. Nick's face leans down towards mine as a member of the football team shouts encouragement of 'get in there, my son'. His breath smells like WKD. I close my eyes and lean towards him, ignoring the increasingly angry shouts coming from the doorway.

A sharp fist grabs my upper arm so hard I wince away from my first kiss, my eyes shooting open.

Gwen!

'Get the hell off her, you massive loser!' she's shouting at Nick who looks like he's been slapped in the face.

The crowds of people laugh collectively at Nick, who is blushing furiously, and move in on Gwen and me. I jerk my arm up and away from my sister's tight grip, batting her accidentally but pretty firmly in the jaw with a stray elbow. Her lip bursts open, spraying me with a shower of blood. Weirdly, for a suspended moment in time, I'm grateful for my wipe-clean dress, before Gwen notices and throws her hands over her mouth to stem the bleeding. I break free. Shouts of 'fight, fight, fight' emanate all around us but this isn't the school playing field, it's Sally Morton's front room.

'Get in the car,' Gwen hisses at me through a swollen lip and clasped fingers. 'Now!'

I drop my head, so embarrassed that I can't even look in Nick's direction and follow Gwen out to where she parked Mum's car in front of Sally's driveway.

We travel back home in silence, but I can feel the anger radiating from Gwen's whole body. Her lip hasn't stopped gushing, despite the wad of scrunched-up napkins she'd found in the car. She doesn't say a word to me as we pull into our own driveway, the house as dark as night. Mum must have ended her party early, so I really would have been the only person waking Gwen up.

Oh no, her interview! Her face!

She's still silent as we walk towards the house. Still silent as she shuts the front door behind us and trudges up to her bedroom. It's two in the morning and Gwen doesn't say a word to me for the rest of that week.

In fact, her kind words dry up completely from that moment forwards.

Chapter Thirty-Nine

'I'm looking for Pops,' I say breathlessly to the hospital receptionist. I've just run from as close to the Accident and Emergency entrance as the taxi driver could get in his car.

'And what's Pops' surname?' the woman behind the counter asks, smiling at me.

'I . . .' I feel stupid as well as flooded with panic now. 'I don't know. He was brought in just now in an ambulance. Suspected heart attack at my house. He's about eighty. Male. Grey hair.'

My hands circle my head as if the receptionist doesn't know where Pops' hair will be found. She types something and looks back at me.

'Are you family?'

'No,' I shake my head. 'He's my gardener.'

Now I feel even worse. I sound like a bourgeois home-owner who's worked their staff into a coronary. The receptionist raises an eyebrow at me.

'I m-mean,' I stammer, trying not to sound like a twat, 'he's a friend. A *good* friend.'

And he has been – I realise while I'm blurting it out to the poor woman trying to help me – one of the most supportive people I've met while I've been back here in Norfolk. And I wasn't there for him when he needed me most because I was off hunting for a dad who couldn't care two hoots about me.

'P-please,' I say, feeling my throat start to seize. 'If you can just tell me how he is doing? You can ask the paramedics if I was there if that helps?'

She smiles at me again and types something else into the computer.

'Here we go, Mr Stafford,' she says. 'I'm afraid I can't tell you anything about a patient who you're not related to, that's only for the next of kin.'

My stomach lurches twice.

'Is he dead?' I can feel my legs wobble beneath me.

'Oh no, dear, sorry,' she says, half-standing out of her chair to check I'm OK through the safety screens. 'We just can't give out information about patients to anyone.'

'Oh, thank God,' I sigh. 'Can I volunteer myself as a next of kin, now?'

She lets out a little laugh, not unkindly.

'That's not how it works, I'm afraid,' she says. 'You're welcome to wait and see if he's admitted onto a ward, if you'd like to? Then you can go and visit him during visiting hours. Take a seat and I'll come and let you know if he's moved, but it could take a while.'

'That's OK,' I say, feeling relieved. 'I don't have anywhere else to be.'

I take a seat in the waiting area and fish around in my bag for my phone. I want to message Nick because he's the only other person I know who cares about Pops, but I have no idea what to say. What happened between us back at his parents' house? Did he pretend to like me, to almost kiss me, just so he can get me back for what I did at Sally Morton's party fifteen years ago? I slump into a chair and shove my phone back in my bag without sending any messages to anybody.

'What an idiot,' I say to myself, realising only too late

that a man with a very swollen foot sitting opposite me had been saying hello. 'Not you. You're not an idiot.'

I look at his swollen, elevated foot and wonder if perhaps he *is* an idiot. He looks away quickly. With nothing outwardly wrong with me I can imagine what's going through his head now. My own, normal-sized foot taps away with a mind of its own and soon the poor man hops away to a different seat. I sigh and take my phone back out, Mum's letters falling to the floor as I do. I scoop them up and look over them again. The handwriting, so like mine, must have been a fluke, pure coincidence that the man who penned these letters had my looping Ys and slanting Ts. Because vest-wearing Dave certainly did *not* write them. Going on his persona, his love letters would amount to a text message missing vowels and asking for a fish supper from 'round the corner'.

So why did Mum have them sewn into her wedding dress?

'Hello, I'm looking for Larry – Mr Stafford,' a harried voice asks at the reception desk. 'He was brought in just now by ambulance with a suspected heart attack.'

I look up. A woman, shaking out an umbrella and pulling off her waterproof hair-cover, looks frantically around the room while waiting for the receptionist to find him.

Mr Stafford?

'Are you related?' It was the same question she asked me.

'I'm his wife,' the older woman replies.

What?

I'm staring at her and trying really hard to overhear what they start to say to each other but my view is blocked by the man with the swollen foot who is hopping towards the water machine. I get up and walk over to the reception window where Pops' wife is sitting. Pops' wife who I thought was deceased. She looks pretty alive to me.

'Excuse me,' I say to her and she turns to me with wide eyes and a trembling mouth painted in the lightest pink colour. 'I'm sorry, but I couldn't help overhear. Are you Pops' wife?'

'Margaret?' she says to me, her eyebrows shooting up. 'Did you find him? Are you the one who called the ambulance?'

I nod and she jumps out of her seat and hugs me. My nose fills with the scent of lavender soap and her raincoat crinkles as she squeezes me.

'Oh, Margaret, thank you!' she cries into my shoulder.

'How is he?' I ask her.

'He's awake.' She moves away and straightens her coat. My back feels soaking where her umbrella has dripped on me. 'We can go through and see him.'

'I'm not allowed yet, I'm happy to wait here until visiting, though. I'm just glad he's OK.'

'Don't be ridiculous!' She puts her arm through mine and now I can feel how thin she is, her age becomes more apparent. 'You'll be coming, too. I need you to lean against anyway. My legs feel all shaky.'

A nurse calls her name and we follow her through security doors to resus where Pops has a bed in a bay. The nurse pulls the curtains aside and ushers us in.

'Just a few minutes now,' she says. 'He'll be moved up to the wards and then you can visit properly.'

She draws the curtain closed again and Pops' wife throws her arms around Pops. He looks frail, half the person I know him to be. The eponymous blue NHS blanket is barely lifted off the bed, that's how thin his legs are.

'Oh, darling, I was so worried about you,' she says. 'Who would I boss around if you were no longer here?'

She laughs lightly. Pops lifts his eyes open and rolls them at me.

'It's OK, love,' he croaks. 'I'm not going anywhere. Not yet. Just a bit of a scare that's all.'

He reaches an arm up out of the blanket and towards me. I have to move forwards so he can reach me, but when he does his hand is as cold as ice. I grip it tightly.

'Thank you,' he breathes, coughing a little.

'I didn't do anything. I wish I had come home sooner, I just . . .' There's no way I'm telling him about the trip to see my dad. This moment is not for me.

'Eloise, love, could you get me a glass of water?'

'I'll need to check you're allowed. There's a big sign above your head that says nil by mouth.' Pops' wife pokes her head out of the curtains and goes off to find a nurse.

'Pops!' I say, perching on the edge of the bed. 'You said your wife was dead!'

He laughs which sends him into a coughing fit.

'I never did,' he protests as he gets his breath back. 'I just said I like to spend my days out of the house because of my wife. You assumed it was because of the memories. It's because of the reality! You heard her, she's all *nil by mouth* this, and *who will I boss around* that!'

The twinkle in his eyes tells me he's not being serious. And the look he gives Eloise when she walks back in empty-handed is still full of love.

'Nope,' she says to him, sitting next to me on the bed, 'nice try, love.'

Her eyes catch my hands and the letters I'm still gripping tightly, forgotten about in the haste to see Pops.

'How do you have those?' she asks, her eyes darting between the pile of letters and her husband.

'They're my mum's,' I say. 'I mean, they *were* my mum's. I guess they're mine now.'

'Maggie, love,' she says, taking the letters from me and flicking through them, making small humming noises, 'they weren't your mum's. They're mine.'

'Pardon?

The curtain around Pops' bed is thrown back with a clatter. The nurse is kind but stern as she guides us out of the cubicle. She gives Eloise the ward name and lets us know we can go and visit him as soon as he's settled. Her words batter against my head but don't permeate through my skull. A whistling older man comes and takes the brakes off the bed and starts wheeling Pops out of Accident and Emergency. I follow Eloise to the hospital coffee shop and sit down where I'm told to, thumping into the chair. A few moments later she puts a steaming mug of tea in front of me and tells me to drink.

'Maggie,' she says, cradling her own hot cup, 'now isn't the best time for either of us, but I feel I owe you an apology and an explanation.'

'OK.' I chew my lip and blow on my tea.

Having never met this woman before, I am more than confused.

'When Larry and I got together he was away for long periods of time with his work and he used to write me little love notes and leave them dotted around the house for me to find.'

That gets my attention.

'Wait, LS, Larry? *Pops* is LS?'

She nods.

'*He* wrote those notes?'

She nods again.

'But I don't understand. What were they doing sewn into my mum's wedding dress?'

Eloise takes another sip of tea as the tannoy over our heads calls out for the crash team in resus.

'I never did see what Elizabeth saw in your dad, not after the way he treated her. I know I shouldn't say that, but she deserved so much better.'

My mind is whirring so hard it hurts.

'How did Mum get hold of your love letters?'

'It was *my* wedding dress. Your mum wanted to have it altered to fit her. She told us she was going to be getting married and we believed that Dave had asked her. I was so excited and I tried not to think about the fact that your dad was already in a serious relationship. We started to organise the wedding, your mum, Pops and me.

'Your Mum and I spoke of all the notes I'd had sewn into the dress for my own wedding day and she wanted to add one of her own. It never got added, though, because unbeknownst to all of us, Dave was never planning on leaving his girlfriend. It broke your mum's heart all over again, then we all lost contact over the years. Your mum went a bit off the rails, I think. She was so young and didn't deserve it. I was so angry.'

'Were you and my mum good friends, then? I don't remember seeing you or Pops at any of her crazy parties over the years.'

'Like I said, we lost touch. It was hard for Pops and me, we didn't want to side with your dad but I guess we had to.'

'But you just said he treated Mum appallingly, made her break?'

'Yes, love,' she says, and her eyes look rheumy. 'But he *is* our son.'

Je veux te dire ce que je ressens maintenant. Je veux que tu le sentes aussi, même après toutes ces années. Parce que mon amour pour toi ne m'a jamais quitté.

I want to tell you how I feel now. I want you to feel it, too, even after all these years. Because my love for you never left me.

Chapter Forty

'He's your *son?*' I blurt it out. 'But that means . . .'

Eloise is nodding.

'But that's . . .' I'm shaking my own head in disbelief. 'Why am I only just finding this out?'

'Elizabeth was a very proud person,' Eloise says, biting her lip. 'She wouldn't accept our help. We tried every day to see you and Gwen, then she got the courts involved so we had to give up. We tried. I'm sorry, Maggie, we really tried. But I think that for all the trying we did to see you and your sister, Elizabeth worked double to get our Dave to pay attention. And we were all butting heads against each other. Then Elizabeth went kind of off the rails because she couldn't accept that Dave wanted a family with someone else. He went and got married, but by this point your mum already had my old dress and I couldn't very well go and get it back, now, could I? She tried her best by you and your sister, but in the end she was so young and so naive that she just did whatever she wanted.'

My shoulders slump.

'She loved you, you know,' Eloise continues. 'But when she took up drinking and partying, I think it took away the pain of being abandoned. And when the pain was gone, she felt free again. It was a vicious circle. I'm surprised she even still had the dress. She told a mutual friend of ours that she'd bagged it away in the attic.'

I screw up my face.

'She told me she'd lost it,' I say. 'When I asked about the possibility of wearing her wedding dress for my own wedding.' I let out a puff of air. 'I didn't even know she was never married. She just brushed off my question like it didn't matter. But when I arrived back at home it was there, right in the middle of her wardrobe. Pride of place. So I assumed she'd been lying to me again. It's not like that would have been surprising behaviour for her.'

'But she probably wasn't lying at the time,' Eloise says, putting her cup down. 'Maybe she left it out for you to find, when she knew she was dying?'

My throat closes all the way up and tears spring back into my eyes.

'Do you think that's true?' I croak.

Her hand covers mine and I can't believe she's my grandmother. I search her face for signs that we are related; the sparkling blue eyes and the paler than pale skin could have been mine, or that could just be wishful thinking.

'Like I said, love, your mum loved you. Larry tried his hardest to get through to her during her last few weeks. He spent days there, helping her out around the house and in the garden.'

'I knew he wasn't a real gardener,' I laugh and interject.

She shakes her own head, laughing. 'No, he doesn't know the first thing about gardening. He just wanted to find out how he could help your mum, after she had died, with you and Gwen.'

'And what did she say? Did she want you two to be involved?' I lean forward in my seat.

'She asked him to keep an eye on the house once she'd gone. She knew you'd be back – I think that was the main reason why.'

This information is filling me with so many questions, I just don't know where to start.

'Look, I'd best be getting back to Larry, he'll think I've done a runner with that cute doctor.' She winks at me. 'Stay in touch, Margaret, love. We're only down the road.'

She takes out a tissue and pen from her purse and scribbles her landline on it. We hug and it feels like the beginning of something that I can grow to love. The hug of someone who might actually care about me because it turns out that I *do* have a family. I skip out of the hospital and flag down a taxi to take me home.

Home.

I have one thing I need to do in order to make it feel like a forever home. One major thing, anyway; there are a lot of extra things I need to do, like damp-proof, fixing the hole in the ceiling, rewiring, replastering. *That* list is endless, yet it doesn't feel so daunting anymore. I'll need to find a job closer to home, P&R can go jump and I can think of many ways in which to be sent my P45. But I'll probably just write that resignation now I've calmed down a bit. Maybe that should feel daunting. But I can get by for a few months on my inheritance and the fact that I don't have a mortgage to pay or a boyfriend sapping me of all my disposable income.

The taxi pulls up into the driveway and I feel all the energy drain out of my body. The last few hours have been exhausting, let alone the last few weeks. So when I see Ed waiting for me at the open door to my own home, a little flame of anger surges inside me. I pay the driver and pull my shoulders back as I approach the man who is about to become my ex, permanently.

'Maggie,' he says, opening the door wider to let me through beside him, 'you look terrible. Come in and I'll make us a cuppa.'

'What are you doing here, Ed?' I plonk my bag on the hallway floor and trudge through to the kitchen.

I just want to be alone to process everything that has happened to me today. My dad, Nick, Pops, my grandparents! It's too much.

Ed flicks the switch on the kettle as I sit at the kitchen table, my legs no longer wanting to hold me up.

'I thought I'd come and help you now Gwen isn't here anymore. I've been looking at local estate agents and there are a few who are free tomorrow to come and value the place,' he says, now standing behind me and stroking my hair.

I shudder. 'Ed! Get off me.'

'What?'

I turn to look at him, at his baby-blue eyes and tousled blond hair, and my heart jumps at the finality of what I'm about to do. My eyes sting with tears.

'Sit down,' I say, biting my lip to stop it shaking.

'What's going on, Maggie?'

'Ed,' I start, as he pulls out the chair next to me and sits, his face greying, 'when you first arrived here, when you came back to sort things between us, you had a load of papers in your hand.'

'Yeah,' he interrupts me, 'I told you, I was looking for matches.'

His grip tightens around my hand.

'No, you told me you were looking for candles. Not matches.'

'Candles, matches, what difference does it make?' He sounds desperate.

'You weren't looking for either though, were you? There was no need for you to be looking for either of them. You hadn't cooked a romantic meal. The lights hadn't gone out. It was an excuse you came up with to downplay what you'd *really* been doing. I thought you'd come back to sort things out between us, but what was the real reason?'

'Maggie, let's not do this now,' Ed says, his voice croaking.

He gets up off his chair but I'm not going to stop asking him.

'Tell me what you were really doing in Mum's study, Ed? Why you really came back?'

'Look, Mags,' he says, rummaging around in his pocket, 'I came back to make things up with you. I told you that at the time. And . . .'

He stops what he's doing and leans on the back of my chair. Before I can stop him, he's kneeling down beside me. My stomach drops through the rotten floorboards beneath me.

'I wasn't going to do this now. I had a whole romantic idea in my head, but what the hell!'

He lifts a huge diamond ring out of his pocket and holds it up to the light. It's at least the size of a large grape and looks like it cost an arm and a leg – which I know for a fact Ed does not have.

'Margaret Burnett,' he starts.

I can't sit here and let him do this. Not now, it's too late. I bundle to my feet as Ed is telling me how he's always loved me.

'Ed stop. Please stop.'

'Maggie, will you do me the honour of being my wife?'

The room stills. Only the drip-drip-dripping of the leaky roof and the swishing of the weeds in the wind can be heard over the rushing of blood in my ears. Ed's looking at me, wanting, waiting. He's been all I've known for the last thirteen years. My world. It would be so easy to say *yes*. To go back to my old life with Ed, to a job that wasn't really the worst in the world, and we could use the money from the house to buy somewhere together finally. To start a family. Maybe I should just say yes.

Chapter Forty-One

Ed is still on one knee on the cracked kitchen tiles. I need to answer his question because if nothing else, that can't be comfortable. I open my mouth and take a deep, bold breath.

'Wait a minute, Ed,' I say, a niggling thought at the back of my mind pushing forwards and expelling my brave breath in one fell swoop. 'Did you say you've contacted estate agents to come and value my house?'

'Well, no. I mean, I did, yes. But that's not what I just *literally* said, Mags. Did you not hear me when I asked you if you'd marry me?'

I laugh. I don't mean to, but I can't help it.

'You don't want me, Ed. You want *this*,' I say, throwing my hands up and indicating the house.

I get up and walk over to the work surface, hauling myself up on it, my legs dangling over the broken dishwasher. Ed looks like a lost puppy, not quite sure what to do with himself.

'You told me that we could pay off all our debts with Mum's savings, and that we could buy our own house with money from this place. How did you know?'

'What? What do you mean?' Ed stumbles over his words. 'It's obvious the house will be worth something.'

'Yes, OK,' I concede. 'But it's not obvious how much Mum had saved. How did you know we could use her savings to pay off our debts? Our thousands of pounds of debt that *you* racked up by being totally incompetent with money. Even *I* didn't know how much Mum had saved. I thought she'd have spent it all on alcohol. So why did you, a person who only knew my mum as a party animal, not think that, too?'

Ed pockets the ring and squares up.

'OK, so maybe I did see her bank balance when I was looking for candles but that doesn't mean I came back for your money. I love you, Maggie.'

'I'm sorry, Ed. It's too late, I realise that now. You should go back to Annabelle.'

'I told you Annabelle left!' Ed is getting angry now.

'No, what you said was *you* left *her*. It's always going to be the same with you, Ed. Nothing is your fault, the world owes you a favour. Maybe it's a good time for you to be on your own so you can start to take some responsibility for once.'

His whole body sags in front of my eyes, and even though I know I am doing the right thing, it hurts to see him hurting.

Be strong.

'But you can't do this to me! I don't have *anything*. I can't afford the rent on my own and how am I supposed to pay for the rest of this?' He pulls the ring back out of his pocket and points it at me accusingly.

'Wait,' I say. 'You were expecting me to pay for my own engagement ring?'

'No, I thought we could use some of your mum's money.'

'*My* money, Ed.'

'But you always said you wanted a big diamond.'

'I used to think I did,' I say, nodding. 'But I guess we can both change our minds about things, hey?'

'This house has changed you,' he spits 'Having this money has changed you.'

'I don't have any money yet! No, Ed. What *you* did to me changed me. And I thank you for it now. I want a relationship where I'm not always walking on eggshells so I don't annoy you, where I can grow as a person with someone who treats me as an equal. A ring would have been nice, but I'd rather be in a grown-up relationship with a man who can take responsibility for his own actions. I think you should leave, Ed. And I think you should take that ring with you.'

Chapter Forty-Two

'You know,' I say, as Phillip lays the pizza boxes down at the kitchen table and Perdita pops open the wine, 'I have so much to tell you guys about since the last time I saw you and I don't really know where to start. But one thing I can say is: I am staying here!'

Perdita screams and the wine sploshes onto the table. She runs around and hugs me while Phillip claps his hands together.

'In your house?' he asks. 'You're moving home?'

I shrug and glug my wine.

'I'm not sure. I'll need to run it past Gwen first, if I can do that without actually talking to her. But if I can figure out a way to get some money together to buy her out then I will. I feel at home here. In Norfolk, I mean. Plus, my job in London pretty much gave me the heave-ho!'

'Yes!' Phillip raises his glass in a cheer. 'To Norfolk.'

'Fuck's sake, guys, am I going to have to move back, too?' Perdita asks, clinking her glass against mine.

'I think that's only fair, isn't it?' I say, smiling at her.

We each grab a slice of pizza and silence falls on the room as we eat. I don't know what I would have done without my friends over the last few months. Or ever. They're my rocks.

'I may actually have another reason to move back closer to home,' Perdita says, hiding her face behind her wine.

'Or at least buy a weekend pad – I'm not sure I'm ready to leave London just yet.'

It could be the first time ever I have seen her blushing.

'What?' Phillip and I say in unison.

'I think I might be what you guys call *in love*.'

We all squeal a little now and I feel a happiness bubble inside me.

'The back-cracking man?' I ask.

'Yep,' she says and the light in her eyes is proof enough that she is feeling happy.

'We can do triple dates,' Phillip says, excitedly. 'Me and Sam, you and acupuncture man, and Maggie and . . .'

He looks at me and cocks his head.

'You and who, Mags?' he asks.

'Me and nobody,' I say, and I genuinely feel OK about it. 'Turns out Ed only came squirming back into my life to get his hands on my inheritance so we're better off apart. Nick and I may have had a moment – I thought he was going to kiss me, and I was so ready to kiss him back, but he pulled away and I haven't heard from him since. It's OK, though. I think I need some time to sort through other things without worrying about who I'm going to kiss and who is going to break my heart.'

'Go, girl!' Perdita cries. 'You're so strong. You're like Superwoman.'

'Not quite,' I say, picking a bit of pineapple from my pizza and sticking it straight into my mouth. 'I feel like I need a year of sleep to just get over the last few months.'

'But you got through them and that's why you're super,' Phillip adds.

'Let me tell you about my new grandparents,' I say, and I think if Perdita hadn't just swallowed her chicken dipper, she might very well have choked on it.

Chapter Forty-Three

I'm greeted by a full-on sunbeam flirting through the gap in the curtains and dropping into my eyes. It highlights the cracks in the walls and the damp patches just below the window, but I don't mind either of these because, as of today, the house is officially mine and Gwen's. The government machinery has gone through Mum's will and papers and granted us probate so I am now officially a homeowner.

Yes, it may be a decrepit old house with a shedload of work needing doing, but at least it's my shedload. Half mine anyway. In the few weeks that have passed since Gwen left, Ed left, and Nick left, I have managed to strip a wall of paper in the living room and rip out most of the downstairs carpets. I've seen more of my best friends than I can count on all my digits and it's been like we never left each other. Even Pops and Eloise have made it a regular thing to come in and see me here, though Pops is only allowed slimline tonic, no alcohol, and especially no caffeine. I see what he means about Eloise now; as caring and kind as she is, she has a mouth on her that never keeps quiet even when she's eating.

The first time they came to see me, once Pops was discharged from hospital, I was scraping some stubborn woodchip wallpaper from the pantry wall and I was stuck holding a steamer in one hand and a scraper in the other.

Pops took a seat at the kitchen table and Eloise came to see if she could help me. After half an hour of waiting for her to finish talking, Pops came over and took her by the arm, gently guiding her to the table and his own listening ear. I think I learnt more about her bunions that day than necessary, but I loved it. I love every time they come in to see me. We are learning more about each other. And I am learning more about my mum. How she had a wicked sense of humour, how she used to paint, how she used to care for both her parents until they passed on. And how she was ground into the dirt by my dad until she had lost all sense of who and what she was.

A knock at the door sends me flying out of my reverie in bed and into my dressing gown. I tie my hair up as I'm descending the stairs and hope that my face isn't too dribbly or marked with pillow lines as I pull open the door with a little glimmer of hope that Nick might be standing on the other side.

'Oh,' I say, pulling the door open to come face to face with Gwen.

She gives me an almost smile and walks in.

'Good morning,' she says, looking up and down at my dressing-gown clad body.

'Yes,' I reply and follow her through to the kitchen.

This morning had started so well, too. I flick the kettle on and fill the coffee pot.

'No gardener today?' she asks, peering out of the window at the newly mown lawn. 'He's finally made himself useful, then?'

Pops hasn't been allowed in to do the garden, he's not well enough yet, and I'm not sure his wife would let him. Plus, he doesn't need the pretence of tending to the weeds to come over and see me anymore. So I'd hired a ride-on lawn mower and taken down most of the lawn as the flowers had died away for the winter. There's a large wild patch left at the very bottom of the garden, but other than that it's looking pretty good, even if I say so myself. Trust Gwen to imply the exact opposite, though. I grit my teeth.

'About the gardener, Gwen,' I say, pouring us both a cup of strong coffee, 'I think you might need to sit down for this.'

I take a moment to notice Gwen as she brushes imaginary crumbs from one of the chairs at the table. Her face is bare, making her look a lot younger than her thirty-five years. A small patch of darker hair runs down her parting and there's a minuscule stain right in the middle of her sweatshirt.

She is human after all, I think, choosing not to point these things out to my sister because, infantile as it may be, I want to be the better person.

'What is it? Has he sown the wrong grass seed?' She picks at some of the scratches in the surface of the table with a fingernail.

I sit opposite her and put a cup down in front of both of us.

'He's our grandad,' I say bluntly, because this is not a conversation that can take beating around the bush.

Gwen's already pale face fades to see-through. '*What*?'

'I found him, our dad. After you told me his name, I searched for him and he wasn't that hard to find. As you know. He told me you'd been to his house. Stalking him, I think were his exact words.'

Her mouth opens in a perfect O then closes again without uttering a word.

'Oh, don't worry, Gwen, I didn't say anything to scare him off more than he already was. In fact, I don't particularly want anything to do with him. He is a horrible, self-centred arse who lives with the family he wanted rather than the family that was forced upon him at an early age. I had nothing to do with his deserting us, I know that now. He couldn't have been further from the man I would have wanted as a father anyway. You were right about the Fiesta, only that was his son's.'

'You spoke to him?' Gwen asks, her eyes wide.

'Of course,' I say. 'How else was I supposed to ask him why he'd left me all those years ago and if he'd like to come back to me now? Stupid idiot, really. Me, I mean! Of course he didn't want to come back. It's not like he didn't know where we've been all these years. He could have come back at any time.'

'I've never worked up the courage to speak to him,' she says. 'He's probably right, you know. I have been a little stalkerish, staring at their perfect family from a distance.'

'I wouldn't say perfect family, Gwen. Not unless you want a suburban husband who wears a stained white vest and drinks beers from a can all weekend. Whose son calls women "love", and who drives a cigarette-littered Fiesta finished with a spoiler and a go-faster stripe. That's not you, is it?'

She shakes her head, but I can see her bottom lip wobble ever so slightly.

'That's not me,' her voice is croaky. 'But at least he's part of a family, even if it is one we look down upon. Because who are we to frown at anyone's family? Look at ours.'

I huff out a laugh. She has a point.

'We have a lovely pair of grandparents now, Eloise and Larry. Or Pops, as he so cleverly called himself, and it didn't even click with me.'

Gwen's cup clatters to the table and we both stare at the crack forming slowly, slowly down the edge.

'I'm sorry, Maggie,' she says, eventually, and I shake my head.

'Don't be, it's just a cup. I get that you're shocked. I was, too. It's only china and we have plenty more in the cupboards.'

'No, not for the cup – the cup is hideous anyway. I mean I'm sorry for everything. I thought it was your fault that Dad left. That Mum went off the rails because Dad left. I thought it was all because you came along. I've hated you all these years because I thought that it was all your fault. And the one night I had my escape plan formulated, a job at a Cambridge college that would have come with accommodation and food, you ruined it by punching me in the face.'

'It was an accidental elbow,' I say, looking at the tiny scar running from her bottom lip even now and realising the gravity of what I had done that night. 'And I had no idea that was your escape route. Gwen, I'm so sorry.'

She shrugs, and her hand reaches over the table and covers mine.

'No, please don't apologise to me. You were young and trying your best. I can see that now. And even if it was your fault Dad left – and it might have been, mightn't it? He might have buggered off because Mum fell pregnant with you? But he was never really hers, was he? Never really ours? *He* was the one who was to blame for all of this, but he was my dad and you were easier to heap all the blame on because it all went wrong when you came along. But Maggie, I realise now that I was wrong.'

I can't believe it. Gwen is apologising to me for thirty-two years of anger and pain. Even though over the last few days I have done very little except be over-emotional, the tears once again fill my eyes.

'I am sorry, too,' I say through snotty hiccups. 'I should have been more sisterly, realised what it is you went through, seen that you needed to get out as much as I did. The hurt of what our parents did wasn't only mine to feel. We just felt it in totally different ways. I'm sorry, so sorry . . .'

We look at each other across the table and our faces break into smiles at the same time. I withdraw my hands from Gwen's and wipe away a tear.

'I'd like to stay here,' I say. 'I want to live in Norfolk now; there's nothing in London for me and there's everything here. I understand if you still want to sell this place so you can get your half of the money, but will you let me do it up first so we can get a good price?'

'Stay as long as you need to,' she says. 'We can do it up together – you'll need my eye for the decorating anyway.' A wry smile creeps onto her face. 'And we can think about how we sort out the funds when we're ready.'

'Wow, thank you, Gwen.'

'It's OK; you're more suited to this place anyway. I prefer clean lines and new-builds. Less to worry about.' Gwen sips her coffee and looks around the kitchen. 'That wasn't a dig, by the way, there's nothing wrong with liking things from the olden days. So how is Nick?'

Who would have thought it? Gwen has a wicked sense of humour. I try not to think about the years wasted arguing when, in actual fact, I think our personalities would have blended perfectly. We have each other now and we can build on that over the rest of our lives.

'Nick's AWOL,' I say, shrugging. 'I haven't seen or heard from him for weeks.'

'But you and he had such chemistry! I could tell that and I barely met him.' She makes her hands do a kind of explosion around her head. 'What happened?'

253

'You didn't meet him, you just spied on us from a distance. And I don't really know,' I say. 'One minute we're getting on well, the next he tries to kiss me, and then I think he got scared.'

'He tried to kiss you?'

I nod.

'And you did what?'

'I looked at him, not quite believing it, then got in the taxi to go home.'

'And you've contacted him since to say you'd like to see him again and that he should come over for coffee?'

I wrinkle up my nose as I shake my head.

'Everything happened at once then. Pops . . . everything. I put Nick to the back of my mind, even though he was fighting to be there, front and centre. Some things are bigger than love.'

'Then no wonder he's gone AWOL. He put his heart on the line for you – again – and you haven't reached out to him.'

'I thought maybe he was getting me back for Sally's party, when you dragged me away from him and I left him in the middle of the room without kissing him then, too.' I shrug.

'You're an idiot sometimes, Maggie,' she says, kindly. 'You guys were fifteen. Who on earth would act like a child when they were a fully grown adult just to get someone back for a kiss that didn't happen seventeen years ago?'

'Ed?' I laugh, then stop laughing abruptly when I realise I may have missed the boat with Nick. 'Argh! What should I do?'

'Hope he hasn't hooked up with anyone in the time you've been waiting for him to get back in touch with you. He's a very attractive man. Did he know you and Ed had split up?'

I wrack my brains.

'I don't think Ed and I had split up when it happened,' I say, realising that maybe that's what Nick meant when he said he *didn't do that*. He didn't want me to cheat. 'Then everything just got in the way. Dad. Our grandparents. You shouting at me about the dress and then dropping a bombshell about Dad. I never had a chance to tell him about Ed.'

Gwen grimaces.

'Ah, yeah. About that. Sorry.'

'It's OK, it wasn't Mum's dress anyway, it was Eloise's,' I say, then cringe. 'Oh, shit. I cut up Eloise's wedding dress.'

We get up from the table and run up to Mum's bedroom, laughing at each other as she pushes past me on the stairs. She may have apologised but Gwen will never lose her competitive streak.

'I think it's fixable,' she says, a huge grin on her face as she holds up the skirt with a tiny strip of bodice still attached.

'Ha ha,' I say, screwing my face up.

'Wait,' Gwen says, her own face now as confused as mine, 'what's this?'

She flips the skirt inside out so the toile is over her hands like a giant lacy fountain. Inside, in between two layers of gauze and lace, there's another note.

'You must have missed this one with the scissors,' she says, picking with her nails to free it from the dress.

We sit on the bed together and Gwen reads it aloud.

'To my darling daughters. I'm writing this to you in the hopes that you find this dress. Darling Maggie, it was never mine to give away, I hope you can understand that now. This is a note I am adding to you both. I only

ever wanted the best for you, that's why I never told you about your dad. If you want to find him, then that's up to you — but be warned that he may not live up to your expectations. Let's put that down to my being blindsided by love.

I know I wasn't always the best mum, but I do love you.

And if, one day, you wear this dress, please do so only for a man who treats you with respect and love and kindness and who knows you're actually getting married!

With all my heart, Mum x'

By the time Gwen has finished reading we're both a mess of tears and toile.

'So, she did care . . .' Gwen says, putting the note down out of the way of our falling tears.

'She had a tough time, Gwen. I guess it's time to forgive her, hey?'

She nods, sniffing hard.

'Now all I have to moan about is the fact she gave me the name of an old woman,' I laugh through my tears and snot.

'I don't know what *you're* complaining about,' Gwen hiccups. 'At least you're not named after some sycophantic idiot who makes fanny-scented candles.'

'Gwyneth!!' I say, and I cannot stop myself from laughing as we grab for each other and hug for the first time in three decades.

Chapter Forty-Four

I can't see through the rain battering at the window of the number seven bus as it makes its way through the traffic of Norwich. I've tried to call Nick but his phone is going straight to voicemail and WhatsApps and texts aren't delivering to him. So I've deduced from this that he has either blocked me or dropped his phone down the toilet. I hope it's the latter, though only a clean toilet.

Gwen was right. I need to find Nick and tell him how I feel, now I know how I feel. So getting out on a bus to Norwich is a relief, even if it is tinged with the dread of finding Nick and him telling me he's now married. Yes, it may be unlikely in the three weeks I haven't see him, but stranger things have happened, like the rekindling of mine and Gwen's relationship and the acknowledgement that Mum wasn't as bad as we first thought. Things come in threes, don't they? But then again, I have found a pair of grandparents that I never knew I had, so that's an even three. An odd three? A full three?

I hop off the bus in the city centre and slog it through the crowds to Nick's office. The rain is relentless now and my umbrella is redundant as there are too many people about to risk it. I don't want to take someone's eye out in the pursuit of love and happiness, not even the annoyingly slow people who take up all the pavement. Reconciliation and acceptance have been great for my patience and blood pressure.

I spot Nick's office, tucked away down the cobbled road. It seems like a million years ago I was here with Nick, and the promise of a father. But now I have grandparents and the memory of a mother. And hopefully, in a few minutes, the heart of a man I think I may have loved since I was at high school. Squealing excitedly on the inside only as there are too many people around for obvious emotions, I peek through the window into the office. He's there, at his desk, his back to the wall and his face studiously staring at Susie who is all smiles and happiness.

My heart drops all the way down to my toes that are now soaking wet in my trainers as I watch him get out of his chair and manoeuvre around his desk. They embrace and I shake my head.

I'm too late.

'I'm about seventeen years too late,' I laugh to myself as I turn and trudge back to the bus stop in the torrential rain. For a split second I think I hear my name, but it's probably tyres splashing in puddles so I tuck my head down and keep going, the urge to be back at my house with a coffee is overwhelming.

It's OK, I think. I have a new life to start. A sister to get to know. A mother to relearn memories about. Grandparents who have shown me so much about myself and my history. And a giant house that isn't going to repair itself. That is enough to keep me going. I only hope that Susie treats Nick well this time and doesn't end up breaking his heart. He's a good guy, he always was. I know now that it isn't Nick who has changed, it's me. He was always quietly confident, did his own thing without caring what others thought. He was confident enough to be honest with himself about what he liked: long hours in the library, staying behind after class because he enjoyed the work. Nick never cared about what people thought about him and why would he? He was happy and loved. I, on the other hand, had been a sheep at school. Always craving the validation of my peers because I couldn't get it from a mum who had bottled things up in more ways than one, and a sister who hated me. It twisted me into a person I thought others would like, instead of the person I wanted to be. I had been too scared, back then, to admit to anyone other than my bestest friends that I fancied the pants off the quiet, bookish boy, and now I am paying the price. He's grown into a man who could have anyone he wants. But I have grown, too. And I can continue to grow on my own.

The bus is full on the way home. Condensation drips down the window and rainwater drips off the people. It has the smell of old burgers and feet. I am trying really hard to stay upbeat as I give up my seat for an old woman who has somehow made it up to the top deck and now wants to sit down, but it's getting harder to do so, the fuller the bus is getting.

As the people dwindle, the further out of the city we get, I manage to grab a space right in front of the mouthy teens on the back row. I clutch my bag to my knee and peel out my phone. Scrolling through the photos of the love letters that are now safely back with their rightful owner – though unfortunately the same can't be said for the wedding dress, which *was* unrepairable – I stop to take a moment to read them, wondering if I can match the letters to Nick's translation. There's the first one, the simple 'I love you', the forever yours and the love forever in my heart that I can read because they were the ones I was holding when Nick said those words to me, roses are red, and how when my grandad first caught sight of my grandma he knew he'd found love. I flick between the photos of the letters and Nick's translations. There's the one about being on the other side of the world, the chances they took and how their hands fit together. I reach the end of the original letters and flick back to the translations, my eyebrows wrinkled.

Where's the one about love being easy or the one where Pops tells Eloise how he feels now, even after all these years?

I nearly miss my bus stop as I flick my finger back and forth over my screen, sliding the photos to try and find the missing letters, all the while dread filling my boots as I think I must have lost the last two originals.

Gwen meets me at the door and her luminous smile is infectious.

'You've got a visitor,' she says, helping me out of my mac which has stuck to my skin with the rain and heat from the bus. I cock my head inquisitively and she laughs.

'I've put him in the drawing room for safekeeping.'

'Gwen!' I say, letting my dripping wet hair out of its ponytail and hoping it's too damp to spring up and fill the hallway. My wishes are not granted as my hair triples in size when it's released. 'We're not living in a Jane Austen novel.'

She pushes me by the shoulder blades into the room where this all started, where Mum's funeral had her closest companions, and a few extra, gathering to say goodbye. I haven't been in here since, save for a few quick peeks at the ceiling to make sure it wasn't going to fall in and that the walls weren't riddled with damp. But it had been the soundest room, that was why Gwen and I had picked it all those weeks ago for Mum's wake.

I peer around the door just as Gwen gives me one last shove. Stumbling into the room I see the back of Nick's head as he stares out the window to the rain lashing the driveway, his curls as comfortingly unruly as ever. He hears me as I fall into the room and turns to me, smiling.

'Hi,' he says. 'I hope it's not bad form to be waiting here for you?'

'Nick,' I splutter. 'How? Was that not you in your office with Susie?'

Nick takes a step towards me. I can feel my heart hammering in my chest.

'No,' he says, giving me a cheeky smile, 'it *was* me. Susie came by to pick up some stuff she left.'

'O-oh,' I stutter. And feel stupid and relieved all at once.

He shrugs his broad shoulders. 'Susie and I were just saying goodbye. I saw you through the window and I did try to call after you.'

Not tyres in puddles after all.

'I thought perhaps you were back together and I didn't want to come and talk to you because what I needed to say wouldn't work with your girlfriend there.'

'We're absolutely, one hundred per cent through. I think we have been for a while. She needed her coffee machine back as she's moving in with her new boyfriend. What was it you wanted to say to me?' Nick moves even closer now, but he could be miles away and the energy fizzing between us would still be visible.

I freeze. I cannot move. With my damp clothes still sticking to my skin, and my hair about to get a postcode of its own, I reach out a hand towards him. He makes one final step and the gap between us is closed as he takes my hand in his. His other hand strokes my cheek, his fingers cool on my hot skin.

'That I've missed you,' I whisper.

'I've missed you, too, Maggie,' he says, smiling. 'It has been really hard not getting in contact with you, but I felt that I was getting too close and I needed time and space to work on my feelings for you, feelings that have been there since I was so young and I first saw you walk into my chemistry class with your beautiful hair and the smile you gave me. You made me feel *seen*. But . . . Ed. It wasn't fair on either of us that I was around, muddying the waters when you were trying to patch things up.'

He leaves the unasked question floating in the air.

'Ed and I split up. He was only after Mum's money. *My* money . . . and the house. I have known all this since before you and I went to visit Dave but I hadn't told Ed so I didn't think it was fair to tell you.'

'You have?' he asks, tucking my hair behind my ear.

I nod. 'And that day, when we almost kissed but you pulled away, I thought it was because of me, because you couldn't be tied to one person. Or that you still hated me for what happened at Sally Morton's party.'

Nick's eyes widen. 'No, no, no!' He shakes his head, a small smile curling on his lips. 'What happened at the party wasn't your fault, Gwen dragged you away! Besides, we were only teenagers. Things just got busy after that, A levels and life, and I thought maybe you had gone off me because you didn't smile at me in class anymore.'

'I was too embarrassed.'

He strokes my bottom lip with his finger, sending my skin into overdrive with sensations.

'I didn't kiss you that day outside my house because you had a boyfriend and that would have been wrong. But it was the hardest thing I have ever done. Or not done, in this case.'

262

'Oh,' I breathe onto his fingers. 'Oh! You know, maybe it's a good thing we didn't kiss then. I think I needed time, too.'

I lean my face into his cupped hand.

'So now we're both here, and we're both single . . .?' He gives another cheeky grin, taking his hand from my face and sliding it down my arm to hold my other hand.

'Nick,' I say, realisation flooding my brain, 'those extra love letters. The translations I couldn't find physical copies of. They weren't translations, were they?'

If love was easy, everyone would take it for granted.

I want to tell you how I feel now. I want you to feel it, too, even after all these years. Because my love for you has never left me.

He shakes his head.

'They're from me. To you,' he whispers, and he pulls me in to him. His hands circle around my back and hold me close. 'I wanted to tell you how I felt, that my feelings for you blossomed inside me the moment I walked into your kitchen and saw you there with your mum's wedding dress. I liked you when I was a teenager, Maggie, fancied you something rotten. But now . . . now I feel like I could fall in love with you.'

I stutter out a breath. I feel like I've come home, because it's always been Nick.

He moves his body so he can look down at me. And before either of us can do anything about it, before anyone else can ruin the moment that has been building for almost two decades, Nick's lips find my own and he's kissing me and I'm kissing him back.

And it's just us. Nick and Maggie. A history worth fighting for and a kiss worth waiting for.

Acknowledgements

As *The Love Note* is a book written throughout the pandemic I have to start my acknowledgements with a heartfelt thank you to all the NHS, social care, care, and emergency services staff, the teachers, and all of the key workers who got us through 2020 and are still working their magic now. And to all my colleagues in social care who were a pillar of support despite our increasing workloads, thank you.

To my agent, Tanera, who read the beginning of this book and loved it enough to want to call me, despite it not being finished! Thank you for your support and for being a voice of reason and encouragement all in one kind and friendly bundle. I can't wait until we can meet in person!

A huge thanks to my wonderful Orion editor, Rhea, whose eye for detail and story pulled this book into the best shape it can be.

To the Romantic Novelists' Association, who ran a (virtual) conference in 2020 despite being in the middle of the apocalypse and whose agent one-to-ones made it possible for me to send my manuscript flying over the slush pile and straight onto Tanera's desk, without you I wouldn't be here, thank you!

Thanks to all the people who read early drafts and said enough kind things for me to keep going!

Thanks to my partner and my family, for their unconditional love and support. This year has been hard and I am so grateful for you all.

And finally, thanks to my Gran Baird, who very sadly passed away this year. Thank you for the creative genes and the cheeky wit that thankfully made it all the way down to me!

Printed in Great Britain
by Amazon